Fantastic

Discounts &

Deals for Anyone

Over 50!

"If you are age 50 or better and paying full price, you're paying too much...Your hometown is swarming with discounts, many of them never advertised nor offered unless you ask for them. *What stands in your way?"*

— *From the Introduction*

About the Author

Janet Groene, with her husband Gordon Groene, "retired" while they were in their 30s. They sold everything they owned, bought a sailboat, and went to sea. For ten years they cruised the islands in winter and summered in the mountains in their RV, making a living as a writer-photographer team. They now have a home base in Florida. Their books include *Caribbean Guide* and *Puerto Rico and the Virgin Islands* (Open Road Publishing) and many other books on travel, RVing, food and boating.

Fantastic Discounts & Deals for Anyone Over 50!

Janet Groene

Cold Spring Press

Cold Spring Press

P.O. Box 284
Cold Spring Harbor, NY 11724
E-mail: Jopenroad@aol.com

ISBN 1-59360-003-8
Library of Congress Control Number: 2003110510

Printed in the United States of America

DISCLAIMER

Discounts mentioned in this book were carefully researched but may not always be available when and where you seek them. Individual franchisees are free to set their own senior discount policies, so the discount you get at one fast food outlet may be different from that of another member of the same chain. The free bank account you're using now may not be free next year. Memberships and mergers come and go. Policies change. Call ahead to clarify if a senior discount exists and, if so, what age you must be and what steps you must take to take advantage of it. The publisher and author cannot be responsible for disparities, discontinued discounts, or disappointments.

Table of Contents

Introduction

Age is only a number. So is ten, as in 10% off and 50, as in Free Checking Account for people aged 50 or better. How about a free soft drink with your meal at a fast food restaurant? Up to 40 percent off your hotel bill? A discount on your next lube job?

If you are age 50 or better and paying full price, you're paying too much!

Your hometown is swarming with discounts, many of them never advertised nor offered unless you ask for them. *What stands in your way?*

Perhaps you never think of asking for a senior discount. Or you're proud, or embarrassed, or you don't want anyone to know your age. OK, but we know airline pilots and business executives who snapped up an AARP card as soon as they turned 50. Many people ages 50 and up routinely finagle a senior discount as often as possible. The savings are *yours for the asking* – so ask!

If embarrassment is a problem, get the discount as discreetly as possible. The most obvious way is simply to phone ahead, which is a good idea anyway to (1) confirm that the business does indeed give a discount and (2) to verify rules about which age the discount kicks in and what you must do to get it. Get the name of the person you spoke to in case there is a dispute later. Now, all you have to do is to ask quietly for the discount when you take the car in for service or order your restaurant meal. When reservations are involved, such as renting a car or booking a hotel, proof of age must be shown at check-in. Cruise ships and airlines require photo ID from everyone. You may also need a membership card such as AARP, Senior Wings, Golden Age, or Monday Club.

According to the American Hotel and Motel Association, seniors spend 4.9 nights away from home when they travel, the longest period in the travel industry. Almost 20 percent of their trips last seven nights or more. As a traveler aged 50 or better, you're the darling of the hospitality industry. You have buying power, available time, and strength in numbers. But hotel and travel discounts are just the beginning. Read on.

BE PREPARED
Most of the discounts mentioned in this book don't just fall into your lap when a clerk sees silver threads among the gold. You have to seek them out, meet all the rules, and make sure you get every darned dime you're entitled to. Here's how:

•Be prepared at all times to show proof of age when you ask for a senior discount. You might, for example, negotiate a senior discount when making hotel reservations by phone but, as mentioned above, you must be prepared to show proof of your age at check-in.

•In addition, be prepared to show any other cards that are involved in your discount, such as your AARP membership or Applebee's Golden Apple Card. Some deals, especially over the phone or on the Internet, also require you to give a discount code that is printed on a membership card.

1. Senior Savings A to Z

Hitting 50 is a shocker. Worse still, aftershocks keep coming as you pass 55, then the big 6-0. In two short years you'll be 62, wondering if you should take Social Security early or wait until you can get full benefits. In a flash, you'll reach the traditional retirement age of 65. Yet you still feel 49, maybe even 29. The last thing you want now is for co-workers to see you as over the hill, past your peak performance. If you're still in the dating game, it's even worse if you don't want your love interest to know your real age.

However, there are compensations for getting older, many of them monetary. Senior discounts start kicking in when you turn 50, especially if you are a member of **AARP**, the American Association of Retired Persons or **CARP**, the Canadian Association of Retired Persons. More discounts are yours at age 55. Even more are available when you turn 60 and 62, and almost every senior discount applies to those aged 65 and over.

Start by asking your hairdresser or barber, who already knows that you touch up the gray, when you can start getting a senior discount on salon services. (It may be 55, 62 or higher). Then just sit back and wait for discounts to mount up as the years roll by. If you want to keep your age a secret, go ahead. Nobody's going to force you to pay less. In fact, senior discounts probably won't even be mentioned unless you bring them up.

The first rule of getting the most for your money is to stay sharp, up to date, informed, and relevant. Read at least one daily paper and all the free shoppers you can lay your hands on. Listen to a local radio station for local news. Read bulletin boards. Network. Schmooz with other seniors to find out what's new.

Accept the fact that the Internet is here to stay, and is the place to find coupons, discounts and savings that may be unavailable anywhere else.

Master it. Harness its power to comparison-shop for everything from insurance to a new car and to learn what new discounts are available on your next trip (but don't be suckered into thinking the Internet is the only place to find discounts, or the best one). With each birthday, savings mount. If you don't want to buy a computer, use one at the public library, where free courses in computer use are also available. An hour a week online should be enough to keep current on the Internet senior discount scene.

Here are some ways to save money at age 50 and better:

•Stay on the ball by reading your local newspaper, at the library if necessary. Here you'll find news of free programs such as celebrity author book signings at book stores, free recitals at the local university by tomorrow's opera stars, movie or TV filmings with free tickets, lectures by visiting luminaries at local colleges, churches and clubs, and much more. Often, free recitals at churches and synagogues are open to members and non-members alike. Many feature internationally known artists.

•In recent years, state and local taxes have edged up faster than almost any other living costs. When figuring a 15% tip, compute according to the cost of the food, not the total bill after taxes are added. A $25 lunch for two, for example, calls for al $3.75 tip at 15%. The same lunch, taxed at 13% for a total of $28.25, could prompt an unwary tipper to pony up as much as $4.60-$5. Out of fairness to the server, however, do figure the tip on the full, pre-tax price of the meal before the senior discount was subtracted.

•Pick up free booklets and "shoppers" everywhere you see them. They're filled with two-for-one restaurant deals, dollars-off haircuts, freebies and discounts. Most mass market stores and supermarkets have a special rack at the entrance where stacks of free publications can be found.

•Grab free senior newspapers found in doctors' offices and at business waiting rooms. In one issue of a free, senior tabloid published in east-central Florida, we found coupons for 10% off a massage, $3 off dinner at one of the area's better restaurants, 35% off watches, 20% off any jewelry purchase, and announcements of several health fairs where free screenings and checkups were being given. Two theaters advertised senior discounts on tickets plus a free box of popcorn at one and, at the other, free popcorn with the purchase of a drink. Coupons are a way merchants use to gauge reader

---

About AARP

It's one of the most powerful lobbying groups in the United States, a powerhouse known not just in the halls of Congress but throughout the business community. Whether or not you agree with their political agenda, AARP membership can be a plus. For those aged 60 and over, many advantages apply but if you're aged 50-59, membership is almost a necessity because many of the best discounts for that age group are available *only* to AARP members. An added plus is that a spouse of any age can go along for the ride. If one or both of you are 50, you probably never think of yourself as senior citizens. Yet this one little card can save hundreds of dollars a year on lodging, car rental, mobile home insurance, prescriptions and much more. Shop and compare because auto clubs, which offer many of the same perks, are not age-related and may carry advantages that AARP does not. Membership in AARP is available to those aged 50 and over. The cost is $12.50 for one year, $21 for two, and $29.50 for three years. At the same rate, there is a special division for active and retired educators. The address is AARP, Membership Center, P.O. Box 93109, Long Beach FL 90809. *Tel. 800/424-3410.*

---

participation. Patronize those who support local seniors, and save a few bucks in the bargain!.

•From the day you turn 50, always ask, ask, ask about senior discounts. They are almost never offered voluntarily.

DISCOUNTS FROM A TO Z

Note that discounts can vary greatly even within the same chain. Use the following as a guideline, but always verify in advance and make sure you understand all the rules, blackout dates, age limits, and limitations. If you don't, you might be disappointed at best or, at worst, embarrassed by a loud and deliberate turndown.

Airline discounts for seniors are like the old gray mare. They ain't what they used to be. However, some deals are still available not just for seniors but for companions of any age. See Chapter 4.

FANTASTIC DISCOUNTS & DEALS FOR ANYONE OVER 50!

Almost every service and merchandise is available at a senior discount in communities that have city-wide senior discount programs in which merchants cooperate with a senior center or service club. Call your senior center, Council on Aging, or Chamber of Commerce and ask. In Glendale, California, for example, senior discounts are available on everything from accounting to floor covering. Participating merchants set their own ages and rules, which are available from the agency that sets up the program. More about that in Chapter 7.

Americans in Canada get a big discount immediately because, at this writing, it costs only about U.S. $.70 to buy one Canadian dollar. In addition, Americans visiting Canada can get a refund of the Goods and Services tax (GST) that Canadians pay on everything they purchase. It's similar to the VAT in England or state sales taxes in the U.S. The tax is collected from everyone, so save all your receipts to claim the refund later. Hotels and shops have the rebate forms on hand; instant cash rebates are available at some Canadian Duty Free Stores. Rebates apply to hotel taxes for stays of under 30 days, and for goods amounting to $50 or more. Make your claim as you leave the country. If you're in and out of Canada often, as are many Americans who live close to the border and do much of their shopping in Canada, you can accumulate receipts and make a single claim yearly through the mail-in program. For information, call 800/66-VISIT (668-4748) from anywhere in Canada.

Amtrak generally offers a discount of 15% to seniors aged 62 and over. Additionally, the Oregon Department of Transportation supports Amtrak Cascades passenger train service between Eugene and Portland OR, including stops at Albany and/or Salem, with a $5 round trip fare for groups of 20 or more. (Companions can be any age.) Get your friends together and plan an outing! Information and application forms are available on this Oregon DOT website, odot.state.or.us/rail/SENIOR%20TRIPS%202002-2003.pdf. Nationwide, contact Amtrak at 800/USA-RAIL or www.amtrak.com.

Auto Racing. Be a part of this exciting sport by sponsoring a race car. If you're a businessperson aged 50 and over, sponsor an Angelo Taylor racing car at a 50% discount. Your ad on the car and/or the driver's clothing will be seen by hundreds of thousands of race fans. Visit www.angelotaylor.com

Auto Repairs are sometimes discounted for seniors (see Chapter 7), so ask–preferably after you get a written quote for the service so they can't pad the estimate. It's also a plus if the repair shop offers pick-up, or a ride home after you have dropped off your car. For example, Scottie's Auto Repair in Hillsboro OR offers local seniors both a discount and a ride. Tel. 503/648-4275. Call around your city. It's likely there's a big-hearted Scottie in your town too.

Ballet performances usually discount tickets for seniors. Check the price schedule for individual tickets. Senior discounts may also apply to season tickets or membership, giving you a double dip.

Beauty Salons often offer a senior discount across the board or on certain services on certain days. For example Universal Hair Bazaar in Tuskegee AL offers a 10% discount to seniors and Plait 'Num Braids in the same city takes $5 off a senior's bill. Call around and ask. A salon near you has a deal for seniors.

Botanical Gardens worldwide offer a senior discount, free day or free hours. If you visit a local garden regularly to see the ever-changing botany show, look into an annual membership. It's usually discounted for seniors. With membership, you get free or deeply discounted admission every day.

Bus and Inter-urban fares are discounted for seniors but each municipality has its own rules. You may have to buy a special pass or sign up for special ID issued by the bus company. Ages vary according to the city. LYNX in Greater Orlando, for example, allows seniors 65 and over with ID to travel for 25 cents single fare or to buy passes for unlimited rides. MTA in Greater Los Angeles lets seniors ages 65 and higher ride for $12 monthly and people aged 62-65 who are not employed full-time to buy passes at a discount. In New York City, bus and subway passes are an excellent buy for people ages 65 and over, but you have to present yourself for a photo and get a special ID that is used just for transportation. Different rules apply to airport buses.

New Jersey Transit gives seniors ages 65 and over a big discount on locals but they pay full price for express buses. Details are available in every city from local drivers, ticket kiosks and service centers.

A special program in Beverly Hills allows seniors aged 62 and over to ride free on supermarket shuttles on Tuesdays. For information go to To see if a similar shuttle or ride is available in your area, contact your local senior center. Seniors who have no other way to get to the supermarket or doctor can also get transportation through groups that pick up in a special van, bus or car.

Car Wash is a local service and we haven't unearthed any national chains that give a senior discount. However, discounts abound at the local level. Call around and ask. Usually the discount is 10% and it's offered only on certain days or during certain hours.

Credit. A penny saved is a penny earned, so you'll "earn" a dollar for every $100 charged to your NestEggz MasterCard. There is no annual fee for the card, which was especially designed for people with retirement accounts, and at press time the interest rate is a modest 8.9%. If you do not get cash advances and pay each month's bill when it's due, there are no further fees. Best of all, a 1% cash rebate goes directly into your retirement savings program. For some purchases, the kickback is even higher.

For example, guests at Marriott's Residence Inn get an 8% payback when they charge their stays to this MasterCard. Harvest House food stores pay back 7%; purchases from Hammacher Schlemmer store or catalog give back 6%; Eddie Bauer stores and catalog buys rebate 4%, and you'll get 3% back on purchases at Pep Boys and 800/FLOWERS. For the full list, see the website, which also contains printable coupons, most of them from familiar chain supermarkets. The entire coupon rebate goes into your retirement account. How much do you spend a year on food, fuel, and all the other things that can be charged to a MasterCard? Multiply by at least 1% plus grocery coupons, and the total is impressive indeed. Tel. 866/438-6262, www.nesteggs.com.

Greyhound gives a 10% discount to people ages 55 and over. Tel. 800/231-2222, www.greyhound.com. Ask too about multi-day passes, which allow unlimited travel in a certain area, such as Florida, for a specified time, usually a week or two.

Canadians in the United States should be alert for Canadian At Par days, which are offered by entire communities and regions as well as by individual hotels and attractions. Usually they're seen in winter, when they're aimed at the many Canadian retirees who spend the entire season in the Sunbelt. Canadian dollars, which are worth only about U.S. $.70, are accepted at full U.S. dollar value, which adds up to a whale of a discount. We don't know of any site you will find one-stop shopping for all available Canadian At Par Days and deals, but watch hometown newspapers in Canada and pick up publications aimed at Canadians in popular wintering spots such as Florida and Texas.

Car care providers often offer a senior discount on labor only, parts only, or some special service. The deal may be available only during certain hours or on certain days. If your break down on the road and must have emergency work done or buy a new tire, ask if a senior discount is available. It may not be, but you have nothing to lose. In your home town, watch ads and call around to get an idea of what perks you might get. For example, Krown Rust Control Centres in Canada usually knock off $10 for senior customers.

Contractors often advertise a senior discount. It can be a bonanza or ballyhoo depending on the integrity of the company. Get a price quote first, then ask how much will be shaved off. Discounts can apply to remodeling, construction, new windows, additions, painting, electrical work, air conditioning, and home construction.

Dance lessons are often offered free or at a very low rate for the first, trial lesson. Beware of long-term contracts.

Dentists often offer seniors a price break. Check your local Yellow Pages first, looking for dentists who advertise that they give a senior discount. Next, try Tel. 800/577-7322. This is a nationwide dental referral service that will tell you only about their members, who pay to be represented by the service. Members have been screened, are listed by location and specialty, and you'll be asked if you need routine care or if this is an emergency. Dentists referred, however, are not necessarily the closest, cheapest or best qualified for your needs.

Once you have names, start comparison shopping. It's difficult for a lay person to compare apples to apples when dealing with complex dental procedures, but you might ask the cost of a normal checkup with full-mouth X-rays or the cost of a normal cleaning. Even if you see one dentist faithfully, you might also shop around for specific needs such as a gold crown, a titanium implant, a full set of dentures, and so on. In getting quotes, however, be aware of hidden extras. The cost of a gold crown may not include prepping the tooth, fitting the crown, or other surprises.

Dry Cleaners may offer a senior discount across the board or on certain garments or certain days. Brown's Cleaners in Ontario, for example, take off 15% for seniors and 20% if they pay in advance. Call around your city and ask.

Eye Care remains an expense for seniors, even those who are on Medicare, because ophthalmology care is covered but not glasses, sun glasses, medications and much more. If you are an AARP member and have a Pearle Vision Center in your area, check out their deals on prescription glasses. Not all franchises participate in the AARP senior discount program, but savings are claimed to be up to 60%. Tel. 888/352-3924, www.pearlvision.com.

Factory tours are entertaining and often free, and many times you leave with a free sample such as a beer from the Busch company or a chocolate from Hershey. Other plant tours involve tight security, protective wear such as a hard hat, and perhaps tram transportation through a working factory. As a result, admission may be charged, and here's where the senior discount comes in. The Mercedes-Benz Visitor Center in Tuscaloosa AL, for example, puts on a boffo show as visitors pick their way through a very busy, fully functioning car factory. It's awesome to follow the creation of a car starting with bits and pieces and ending with a shiny Mercedes that drives away. It's so popular, reservations are a must. Tel. 888/286-8762, www.bamabens.com. Admission is $5 adults and $4 for seniors and children over age 12. Don't take children under age 12. For admission on industrial tours in your hometown or in areas you are traveling, contact chambers of commerce or convention & visitor bureaus.

Fairs are as senior-friendly as apple pie, an old-fashioned midway with blue ribbon for the best canned peaches and the healthiest hogs. Seniors can count on discounted admission to any county or state fair in the nation. Rides, hot dogs and the shooting gallery are, however, rarely discounted.

Ferries are as much a part of the public transportation system in some areas as buses or subways are in others, and are just as senior-friendly. In British

Columbia, for example, BC residents who are age 65 and better can ride free Monday through Thursday. Seniors must show a BC CareCard as proof of age and residency. Seniors who ride the Martha's Vineyard and Nantucket Steamship Authority ferries can buy a book of 10 tickets for $27.50 compared to $44 for regular adult fare.

Fishing licenses are discounted by most states, usually for state residents only. Ages vary, usually kicking in at age 62 or 65, often younger if you're a veteran or a military retiree. Disabled persons of any age also get a discount, which may be parlayed by those who are both disabled and over age 65 or a disabled veteran over 65. Check with the license bureau in your home state and, if you're applying for a fishing license when visiting another state, always if a senior discount is offered.

Fitness Centers usually offer a free trial visit or period, but beware of pressure to sign you up for a long-term commitment. See Sports, Chapter 10 for the inside story on fitness centers that have special deals for seniors.

Flying lessons are a lifelong dream for some seniors, who finally have the time and money to work towards a pilot's license. Check the Yellow Pages for flight schools, then call around to find one that offers a free or highly discounted trial lesson. Although airline pilots must retire at age 60, thousands of pilots go on flying for fun and profit into their 70s and 80s. Instructors find that people aged 50 and over often make the quickest and best students of all.

Fuel. The fuel company best known for its customer loyalty programs is Flying J, a national chain of truck stops that also sells automotive gas and diesel. The chain is a favorite with seniors who travel by RV because Flying J truck stops have good food, hot showers, and allow free overnight parking. With the RV Real Value card, buyers get a discount of one cent per gallon of diesel with a minimum 20-gallon purchase, one cent off each gallon of gasoline regardless of the amount, and five cents off each gallon of propane. For non-RVers, the Flying J Rewards Club provides the same fuel discounts. Application is free and members get a long list of perks including discounts on merchandise and meals at Flying J truck stops, discounts on insurance, special phone cards, and much more.

Once you sign up, simply use your card for everything you buy at Flying J.

FANTASTIC DISCOUNTS & DEALS FOR ANYONE OVER 50!

The more you buy, the more you save. If you travel a lot on major interstates or have a Flying J near you, consider become a Flying J card holder. Tel. 888/ 438-3537 or www.flyingJ.com. Address: Flying J Corporate Office, 1104 Country Hills Drive, Ogden UT 84403.

Gambling is now legal in some form in almost every state. While seniors don't get a price break in state lotteries, they are welcomed with open arms at casinos and high-stakes bingo centers on Indian reservations. Check ahead for special days when seniors get extra chips or drawings, senior discounts for drinks or meals at casino restaurants, a discount on Bingo play, and even free transportation from your hometown to the reservation. For example, Point No Point Casino in Washington has Senior Days every Tuesday and Thursday from 8am-4pm. Gambler Gold Club members who are 55 years of age and older eat at the buffet for half off and are entered in a monthly drawing with two prizes of $250 each. They also get double points for slot and play. Points, in turn can be exchange for cash.

If you're 55 or better, Atlantis Casino Resort in Reno offers 10% off at Toucan Charlie's Buffet & Grille, which is open for breakfast, lunch and dinner including a steak and seafood buffet Friday and Saturday and an award-winning champagne Sunday brunch. People of any age can also sign up for Club Paradise, Atlantis' gaming card, which is good for shows, hotel stays, and dining. The resort is in the heart of Reno's shopping and dining district. Tel. 775/825-4700 or 800/723-6500, or www.atlantiscasino.com.

Group Travel especially for seniors is a specialty of Grand Circle Travel, which also offers packages for grandparents and grandchildren. Since 70 percent of their clients are aged 70 and better, you're assured of good value although there is no senior discount per se. The company travels worldwide ashore, aloft, and afloat, and has a high repeat business. Itineraries are aimed at experienced travelers who can take advantage of low rates in the "off" seasons. Tel. 800/248-3737, www.gct.com.

Health food stores often have a soft spot in their hearts for seniors. Ask about discounts, which are often offered on certain weekdays. Sears Health Food & Fitness Shops in Canada give seniors a 10% discount on regularly priced merchandise, excluding appliances.

Hotel tax rules vary from state to state, but they apply to short-term stays.

In Florida, "short term" is defined as less than six months but may be different in other states. Pay by the night, week or month and hotel or "bed" taxes apply. Rent a home, condo, apartment or campsite by the season and save 6-13% by making a deal for six months and a day. Hotel taxes don't apply to long-term rentals. Innkeepers and campground owners can advise you. Most will also give you a price break for the rental itself, especially if you pay in advance.

Insurance is an enormous labyrinth filled with traps and gaps for seniors. A good driving record works in your favor as you get older because senior discounts are in addition to safe-driver, multi-car and other discounts. Under Canadian law, retirees aged 65 and over as well as younger people who are pensioners must be given a discount on auto insurance. In the United States, State Farm gives a generous discount on its $1 million personal umbrella liability policy to people who are over 50. As you turn 50, 55, 60, 62 and 65, re-evaluate insurance policies and change your coverage as needed. AARP members who take the AARP Driver Safety Program qualify for discounts with many auto insurers in most states. Tel. 888/227-7669.

Interstate snowbirds who go to and from Florida via I-75 can purchase Dave Hunter's Along Interstate-75 and never be without information on the nearest hospital, drugstore, hotel, a motel that permit pets, veterinarian, campground, fuel stop, golf course, or shopping center. The book is published in a new edition each year, 800/431-1579, www.i75online.com.

Malls. Call the mall office ahead and ask what they have to offer for seniors. Sometimes all or most merchants in a particular mall offer a uniform senior discount policy to those who apply for a senior shopper's card at the mall administration office. Stop first at the mall office or information desk and ask because discount policies may not be advertised or posted. For example, the Village Green Mall in Vernon BC has special events when seniors aged 60 and over get a 15% discount on most purchases. While it doesn't have a senior shopper discount, Festival Marketplace in Pompano Beach has something even better for seniors–free valet parking! Shop an enormous, climate-controlled city of more than 800 stores and places to eat without wearing yourself out getting from the parking lot to the entrance. Wheelchair and stroller rentals are also free.

FANTASTIC DISCOUNTS & DEALS FOR ANYONE OVER 50!

Heron Gate Shopping Mall in Ottawa, Ontario has a 60+ club that costs nothing to join. Simply get the card as soon as you enter. **Mall of America** in Bloomington MN is an entire city where one book of discounts applies to many different stores, services and places to eat. Tel. 800/346-4289, www.bloomingtonmn.org, and look into discount packages that include shopping, dining and accommodations while you "do" the mall for several days. **Pointe Orlando**, the dining and shopping center in the heart of International Drive in Orlando has a coupon book that is free to anyone, but you have to ask for it at the mall office. Coupons are good at individual merchants, each with a different offer. These are just a few examples of discounts seniors will find. Check with the main office of your nearest mall.

Massage is sometimes available at a senior discount. Check the Yellow Pages and start calling spas, masseurs and masseuses with the simple question, "Do you offer a senior citizen discount to people who are (name your age)?" One of the best deals we found was at Healing Touch Spa and Massage in Wimberley TX, where people ages 50 and up get a 20% discount. Tel. 512/847-5899.

The Mature Traveler is a monthly newsletter that carries lengthy lists of discounts in special categories. Although it's Internet savvy, it's also a boon to people who prefer a printed newsletter. For subscription information, Tel. 800/460-6676, www.maturetraveler.com. Membership dues are discounted by many social, business and professional groups for people who reach a certain age or have been members for so-many years. Often dues are reduced or free but a cut in status from, say, Active to Active-Retired or Senior may also mean reduced privileges or prestige. Review rules occasionally to see if you qualify for a dues discount and, if so, whether you lose anything in the bargain.

Mobile Home Insurance is available at the best available price through AARP and may be also discounted for seniors by one of your local insurance agents. Call around.

Movies. Most theaters offer a senior price at all showings and another deal that applies to people of any age who attend certain showings, such as those during the 4-6pm time period. Compare. Paying the full "twi-night" rate may be a better deal than a senior discount at 8pm. Deals are local, even among national theater chains, so see what is available in your neighborhood.

Museums worldwide offer a senior discount of some kind. It may apply across the board or only on certain days. At the Pacific Science Center in Seattle, for example, people ages 65 and higher get in free on Wednesdays. If you're a regular visitor to any of your local museums, consider becoming a member. Paid yearly, memberships are usually discounted for seniors and they buy free or highly discounted admission with each visit. Incidentally, some museums are technically free but post a sign that says Suggested Donation in microscopic print, followed by a schedule of prices in big print. Look for this wording, which means you can pay as much or as little as you like. It's an especially common ploy in New York City.

National Parks of the United States sell day and annual passes. If you're under 62, the best deal is an annual pass that costs $50 plus $3.95 shipping from National Park Foundation, P.O. Box 34108, Washington DC 20043, 888/GO-PARKS. Or, if you are an AARP member, get 10% off the annual pass, which is good at all national parks, by calling 888/467-2757. Have your AARP membership number ready.

A Golden Eagle hologram, purchased for an additional $15, can be affixed to the pass to buy admission to other government lands such as Bureau of Land Management, U.S. Fish and Wildlife, and U.S. Forest Service properties. These passes are good for one year. Those who are 62 and over can apply in person at any federally-managed park for the Golden Age Passport, which is good for life. It is good for a 50% discount on admission to all federal parks, historic sites and other federal lands. Camping fees and other charges are additional.

Non-gamblers can eat cheaply at casino restaurants, so don't stay away just because you don't gamble. Gambling subsidizes restaurants, which often operate at break-even or a loss. Some bars and dining rooms at some casinos are off limits except to high stakes players, but most casinos, dog tracks, race tracks and other gambling places have public restaurants where nobody keeps track of whether you bet or not.

Online Shopping is available through senior websites such as www.wiredseniors.com. It takes time to work through the website. Click on the shopping mall, then look for a product line that is of interest. Some senior discounts are automatic when you click on the link from the senior website. Others are yours for the asking. Discounts are modest, usually 5-10%. Other merchants give seniors free shipping or free gift wrap. However, no proof of age is needed.

Prescriptions are a hot issue today. So many deals are available locally and nationally, we don't attempt to cover them in this book. Virtually every national pharmacy chain (Kmart, Wal-Mart, Rexall, Eckerd's, Walgreen's) has some sort of senior deal but the bottom line is what counts. That in turn depends on whether you have insurance, whether you'll accept a generic, whether you are willing to buy in larger batches, and your age. Walgreen's senior discount starts at age 55; AARP's at age 50; others give discounts only to Medicare card holders. Know the name of your medication and the dosage and shop around by phone and on the Internet.

Puerto Rico has special respect for seniors. Events held in public facilities are required to offer senior tickets at half off. Also in Puerto Rico, seniors ages 60 and older may stand in express lines at government offices.

Senior Clubs are a motherlode of discounts from one source. One of the best is Ohio's Buckeye Golden Age Card, which applies statewide. Call local senior centers and ask what's available in your city.

Shakespeare Festivals are found in many areas. Most of them involve an entire season of performances of plays by Shakespeare and others, and sometimes music events and other performances as well. One of the largest and most prestigious is the Alabama Shakespeare Festival, where seniors ages 65 and over can purchase selected seats at half price one hour prior to performance, subject to availability (ID required). Tel. 800/841-4ASF, www.asf.net.

Sightseeing and Dinner Cruises almost always have a deal for seniors. Argosy Cruises in Seattle, for example, offers a huge choice of cruises in the lakes, harbor and locks of the area, and knocks $2 off the price of a lunch or dinner cruise if you're 65. Wendella Sightseeing Boats do hour-long cruises out of downtown Chicago and offer a special price for seniors. When you contact any sightseeing cruise line, ask what senior discounts are available. They may apply only to certain times or certain days.

Sightseeing tours are the best way to start a visit to any new city at home and overseas. Information and perhaps tickets are usually available from your hotel. Often free pickup and drop-off at major hotels is included. Tours are also the most carefree, entertaining way to introduce out-of-town guests to your hometown. Large tours such as Grayline, Key West's Conch Train, St. Augustine's trolley tours and Tampa Bay's Duck Tours usually offer a senior discount. Ages vary, but at Duck Tours discounts begin at age 55. Always ask.

Skiing is more fun for those who are retired and can ski during the week when slopes are less crowded. Check with your local ski centers to learn at what age you can get a discount for lift tickets and skiing. Most start at age 60 and older, rarely 55 and even more rarely at 50. Some discounts don't kick in until age 70. Every ski resort has a different policy. See Chapter 10 for more about ski discounts.

Supermarkets may offer seniors discounts on a certain day of the week or one day a month. Others offer a discount card that can be used for special, senior prices any time. See Chapter 2, Shopping and Banking.

Theme Parks worldwide, with the notable exception of Walt Disney World, give seniors a price break on admission and usually a discount on annual passes as well. Since annual passes usually cost less than regular admission for

---

If You're a Low-Income Senior

The goal of this book is to find discounts for all seniors regardless of income. It is not about receiving Medicaid, food stamps, or disability. However, seniors with substantial incomes may qualify for discounts that are generally thought to be available only to the very poor. The definition of "low income" varies according to your city, county or state, and those who meet minimum income guidelines can get a discount on electricity, gas, property taxes and much more.

Many such guidelines apply only to earned income, not Social Security, so the threshold may be easier to cross that you realize. Additional breaks are available to those who are widowed or blind, regardless of income. In Canada, seniors may also get an exclusion from GST. Call any local senior center and inquire once a year or so. Rules change.

---

three days, they are a bonanza for grandparents who take every visiting grandchild to the theme park or to seniors who visit theme parks often to enjoy the upbeat ambience, ever-changing displays, and magnificent gardens. Age limits vary but start as early as ages 50 or 55.

Thrift shops usually give seniors a discount on one of the slower days of the week. It can often be combined with another discount, such as a frequent shopper's card or a tote bag sale. (They hand you a bag, which you stuff with everything it will hold, and pay one, very low price minus the senior discount.) See Chapter 7, Services, Services.

Travel Agents may offer a senior discount on the cost of their services or may specialize in senior discounts or both. A specialty agency really knows its way around senior discounts, senior-savvy group tours and cruises, and trips that have unique appeal to seniors. Check the Yellow Pages and see if any ads make a special appeal to seniors. If not, call a few agencies to see if they have a senior specialist.

Travel Clubs at the hometown level are a carefree way to travel with a spouse, a friend, or no partner at all. Most communities have them, sometimes as separate organizations and other times under the sponsorship of a bank. A typical chapter of the National Association of Senior Friends has dues of $15 per person or $25 for two at the same address. This entitles members to participate in group trips to dinner theaters, parties, flights, cruises, bus tours far and wide, and attractions. Travels include transportation, some or all meals, accommodations and entertainment, so there are few financial surprises along the way. The best part is having a ride, a designated driver, and a busload of friends to chat with during the ride.

VIA Rail in Canada has a senior fare for people ages 60 and over. Save 10% off the top with additional discounts depending on the destination. You'll also get a free economy class companion ticket for someone of any age.

Veterinarians sometimes offer a discount to seniors. Ask. Senior discounts are also offered by many non-profit spay-and-neuter clinics.

Zoos. Almost every zoo in the world offers a senior discount of some kind. It may apply to everyday admission, or only on certain days. For, example the National Zoo in Washington DC has a special deal the entire month of

September, when seniors receive free parking and a discount in the Smithsonian's National Zoo Stores. On Tuesdays in September, perks are even better because you're admitted to special areas and demonstrations. Another typical deal is offered by Point Defiance Zoo & Aquarium in Tacoma WA and a sister park, Northwest Trek in Eatonville WA. Seniors get in free the third Thursday of every month. Other days, all seniors age 62 and over get a discount and county residents get an even bigger break.

If you're going to any zoo anywhere, call ahead to see if you'd do better by going on a certain day. And, if you're going as a family, look into whether it's cheaper to buy a family ticket rather than piecemeal admission at adult, senior and kids' prices. Do the math. If you go to your hometown zoo often, look into the price of membership or an annual pass. Members or pass holders get in free or at a highly discounted price.

2. Shopping & Banking

In retail, just as in almost every other area of claiming your senior discount, it's almost always necessary to ask. It isn't automatic and, at some stores, seniors must apply for a card that must be presented with each purchase.

Red Alert! It's always best to phone ahead to make sure you understand each store's discount policy. Not all members of the same chain participate in discount programs. The program may recently have been stopped or changed, may require a special membership card, or it may be so under-utilized that clerks aren't familiar with it. Save time, hassle and embarrassment by fully scoping out the discount before shopping a new store.

When calling any business ask if they offer a senior discount, at what age it applies, and exactly when and how it applies. Merchants may make it available but that doesn't always mean they make it easy.

CHAIN RETAILERS
American Men Big & Tall shops are found nationwide, a bonanza for hard-to-fit men who are taller or wider than average. Seniors ages 55 and older get a 10 % discount and, if you're making a large purchase, ask about additional savings.

Banana Republic stores sell trendy clothing, gifts, and everything needed for expedition travel. Many of them offer a 10 % discount to seniors ages 65 and up. Phone ahead; not all stores participate.

Bealls is a Southeastern department store chain that carries clothing, shoes, jewelry, accessories and household decorator items and kitchenware. Gift wrap is free, so it's a boon for seniors who want this chore done for them.

During special promotions, usually about once a month, people ages 50 and over who present proof of age get 15 % off all purchases including sale items. Watch local newspapers. Tel. 800/569-9038, www.bealls.com.

Bealls Outlet stores buy overstocks, samples, seconds, and odd lots and offer bodacious bargains in clothing, accessories and shoes for men, women and children as well as household goods, luggage, small appliances, and other items. You never know what you'll find here, which is part of the fun. You can't be sure of finding your size or a full line of matching separates in all colors and sizes, but goods are new and carry labels you'll recognize. Look carefully, though, because they may be damaged, faded, mis-matched, or mis-labeled. Seniors can sign up for a Monday Club card that is good for a 15% discount on all purchases made on Mondays. Present the card at checkout and it automatically deducts the discount. In addition, people of any age get a card that is punched for every $10 spent. When it's filled with 20 punches, it's good for a 20 % discount on everything rung up on one purchase. Use it on a Monday, and get both the 20 % off and your 15 % senior discount. Tel. 800/569-9038, www.beallsoutlet.com.

Belk Department Stores are a Southeastern chain specializing in name brand clothing, shoes and accessories for men, women and children as well as gifts, household linens, home accessories, and housewares. They offer an exceptionally good selection of giftware that is beautifully gift wrapped. If

---

Using the Internet

Everyone is trying to get rich on the Internet these days, including clever entrepreneurs who establish websites that promise price breaks to senior citizens. Some sites are free; others require payment of dues. While they all promise discounts, most are simply advertising gimmicks filled with pop-up ads for sale prices and deals that people of any age could get. From the senior site, there is a link to a website where you can shop for shoes, medications, clothing or travel at the same prices paid by anyone else. I've checked out dozens of these sites, clicked on hundreds of "special offers" and great deals are rare. One exception is www.seniordiscounts.com, which mentions specific discounts for seniors, city by city. It's an invaluable aid in researching your hometown and cities you expect to visit. Check it often.

---

you like the sample shown, just grab one of the wrapped ones and you're off to the birthday party or shower. On the first Tuesday of the month, many Belk's offer a 15 % rate cut for seniors ages 55 and better. Watch local newspapers.

Bottino's Supermarkets in New Jersey give seniors ages 62 and over a $1 discount coupon. Ask at the courtesy desk.

Bugle Boy clothing stores nationwide are popular with the preppie crowd, so they're a good place to shop for your own duds and for gifts for the kids and grandkids. If there's one in your city, call ahead to see if this store offers a10 % discount to people who are 65 and older.

Carousel Press is a mail-order service that specializes in wholesome books for seniors and families. Mention that you're a senior aged 55 plus and saw this offer in this book, and you'll get a 10% discount plus free shipping. Tel. 510/527-5849.

Charity shops usually have a senior discount one day a week. In addition to **Salvation Army** and **Goodwill Industries** stores, which are found throughout North America, your city probably also has several volunteer-run nonprofits that are found only locally. A typical example is the Pinkie Resale Shop in DeLand FL, which accepts donated clothing, household goods and almost anything else in good condition. Merchandise is attractively displayed and priced to sell; profits benefit the local hospital. On Fridays, seniors get a whopping 50% on everything they buy! Check your local Yellow Pages under Resale Shops or Used Clothing and call shops individually to ask when and how seniors get a discount.

Fair Price food stores offer a 2 % senior discount on Tuesday. Look in the White Pages. If there's a Fair Price in your area, call and ask how the discount works.

Frank's Nursery and Crafts outlets in the Northeast gives a 10 % discount on Wednesdays to seniors aged 60 and over. Check your local White Pages for a Frank's near you.

Goodwill Industries operates thrift shops nationwide, where apparel and goods of all kinds are sold at a big savings. In addition, seniors ages 55 and better get a discount of 10-20 %, usually on certain days. Discounts vary with location. Check your local phone book to see if there's a Goodwill store near you.

Gottschalk's Department Stores are found in more than 70 locations in six western states including Alaska. Known for their old-fashioned service, the stores welcome seniors aged 55 and better to shop on Tuesdays at a 10 % discount. Tel. 559/434-4800 for corporate headquarters, www.gottschalks.com.

Grand & Toy is national retailer of office supplies and stationery throughout Canada. Call your local Grand & Toy to ask about the 10 % senior discount. Tel. 416/445-7255, www.grandandtoy.com.

Groceries are not easy to find at a senior discount because supermarket profit margins are pencil-thin. You might find your favorite supermarket chain in these pages. Check too with local senior centers for names of grocery stores that have a special interest in seniors— sometimes with free delivery, sometimes with a discount, sometimes with both. Food stores most likely to offer a senior discount are small, independent grocers, stores that specialize in health foods or organic foods, and non-profit food co-ops.

Harris Teeter food markets in Tennessee give seniors ages 60 and over a 5% discount on Tuesday.

Hudson's Bay Company stores across Ontario give seniors a 15 % discount on the first Tuesday of each month. The chain is nationwide in Canada; check in other provinces for discount days.

IBM Computers are offered at a discount via www.seniorNET.org, or call: Tel. 800/426-7235, extension 5259.

IGA Food stores are independently owned, so policies differ, but many offer a senior discount on certain days. Look in the White Pages for an IGA near you, then call ahead and ask.

Jo-Ann's Fabrics is a national chain of stores that sell yard goods and all the accessories for home sewing. On Wednesdays, most stores offer a 10 % discount to people aged 55 and up. If there is a Jo-Ann's in your city, call ahead.

FANTASTIC DISCOUNTS & DEALS FOR ANYONE OVER 50!

Kohl's Department Stores is a national chain where discounts of 10-15% are offered if you're 62 and over. Watch ads for these special deals, which are offered irregularly on the occasional Wednesday.

Kroger supermarkets are found throughout North America. If there's one in your city, call to ask if they have a senior discount. At some locations, we found a 5% discount on Wednesdays for people aged 60 and over. At others, we have found 10% on the first Wednesday of the month and at others, people aged 55 or better get a 5% discount. Tel. 866/221-4141 or check your White Pages to find your local Kroger.

Market Place food stores throughout Washington State offer a senior discount on Thursdays. Call ahead and ask. Look in the Yellow Pages under groceries or supermarkets because the stores aren't found under M. Each has its own name, e.g. Smith's Market Place, Brown's Market Place, etc.

Men's Warehouse clothing outlets nationwide specialize in sharp suits, casual wear and accessories from top manufacturers. Find your local outlet in the White Pages and phone ahead to ask if it participates in the 10 % discount program offered people aged 60 and up.

Outlet Stores Some factory outlet stores offer senior discounts one day a week. An example is Factory Card Outlet, 405 North Center Street in Westminster, MD. If there's an outlet complex in your city, call the main office to ask about senior deals. If you encounter an outlet mall in your travels, ask first at the main office. Sometimes individual shop clerks don't know about special, mall-wide promotions.

Publications from On the Go Publications (other than seasonal specials) are offered at 10 % off to seniors. Here's how. Find a list of money-saving publications at http://www.onthegopublishing.com/orderpage.html. Fill out the order and take off 10 % before calculating tax and shipping, indicating that you read about the discount in the Groenes' Fantastic Discounts & Deals book. Shipping charges are calculated at $6 plus 1% of the order. Ohio residents add 5.75% sales tax. Seniors can send a check or money order for the publications or products, along with the order form, to: On The Go Publishing, P.O. Box 91033, Columbus OH 43209.

Ralph's is a large, multi-state supermarket chain that offers a Senior Rewards Card. It brings you special discounts on certain products. New savings can be found every week. We've also seen Ralph's stores that offer seniors aged 60 and over a 5 % discount on Wednesday. Call individual markets and ask.

Ross Dress for Less outlets offer brand name clothing at discount prices every day. Seniors ages 55 and up can lop off an extra 10 % on Tuesdays. Check your White Pages to see if there's a Ross in your city.

Safeway Stores, the supermarket chain in Canada, offer a 10% discount through the Senior Outreach Society, www.senioroutreach.com.

Salvation Army Thrift Stores often have a senior discount one day a week. In Ottawa, Ontario, for example, a 25 % discount is given every Wednesday. Call your local outlet and ask.

Savers thrift stores offer seniors ages 62 a 20 % discount on used merchandise every Wednesday. Check the White Pages for a Savers in your town.

Sears Stores in Canada invite seniors aged 50 and over to join the Mature Outlook Club. Each year, you'll receive hundreds of dollars in discount coupons. Apply at any Canadian Sears store.

Sherwin Williams is a highly respected name in paint, wallpaper and other supplies for the home decorator. Call your local outlet and ask if they offer a senior discount. We've found discounts as high as 20 % for people aged 60 and over who hold one of the Golden Age cards available through senior centers in some cities.

SteinMart is chain of 1,800 high quality discount stores found in more than 30 states, ranging from one store in Iowa to 19 in Georgia, 17 in California and 36 in Florida. Big-name brands in fashions for men, women and the home are sold at a big discount that gets even bigger on Senior Citizens Days. Such days are irregular and infrequent, usually on a Tuesday, when seniors 55 and over get 10 % off the purchase everything including sale and clearance items. Call your local store or watch for newspaper ads. Tel. 888/ STEIN-MART, www.steinmart.com.

Wild Oats Markets are more than 100 natural foods stores found in 23 states and Canada, sometimes under other names such as **Henry's, Sun Harvest** or **Capers**. The everyday senior discount is 5 %, which doubles to 10 % on Wednesday. Deals and days vary by location. At most, you have to be 60 or older but some markets start discounts as early as age 55. For locations, see www.wildoats.com. Or, check your local phone book and phone ahead.

Wolf Camera stores nationwide offer old-fashioned service and follow-up as well as a full line of cameras and equipment. Shop here for everything from the newest camera technology to hard-to-find film for your oldest camera. Ask about the Wolf Pack card for seniors aged 65 and older. With it, you get your choice of a single set of prints, a free second set of prints, or a digital deal.

Zappos.com is online only, but it's a bonanza for hard-to-fit feet. The company carries many famous brands and in sizes from AAAAA to EEEEE. Seniors ages 50 and over get a 10 % discount, but only by special arrangement. Tel. 888/492-7767 to ask how to get the discount.

BANKING

Almost every bank offers a special discount for seniors, but it's important to shop and compare–not just today but every few months. You may benefit by having accounts at several banks and by shuffling savings around to take advantage of the best interest rates. Some deals start at age 50; others kick in at age 55, 60, 62 or 65. Most require that you maintain a minimum balance, such as $100 in checking or $1,000-$10,000 in any combination of money market, CDs, checking, IRAs and other instruments. Understand the rules because you pay fees if you let the balance fall below the minimum even for one day of the month.

The astute senior shopper will compare all the features, which are presented as a bountiful bouquet, then weed out those services that provide little or no benefit. For example, free travelers checks and a discount on hotels and rental cars are worthless if you rarely travel. Another bank might offer a less flashy program but give seniors a bonus rate on their CDs or a preferred rate on an auto loan. Too, "financial planning" services may be free to seniors, but that means only that bankers will do their best to sell you bank products.

A no-fee bank credit card has no appeal if you carry a large balance and are looking for the lowest interest rate, or you prefer a card that pays a kickback in the form of cash rebates or frequent flyer miles. (Discover cards, for example, have a high interest rate but no annual fee and they rebate + to 1% of what you have charged in the past year. State Farm offers a Visa card with no annual fee and a 1% rebate that can be used to pay insurance bills.)

Don't overlook some of the social events that some banks offer their senior club members. Some meet as often as weekly, giving seniors a chance to meet and mingle, play bingo, have a meal at a modest price, or take a day trip to a museum or theater. Small, regional bank groups also sometimes organize discounts at local businesses and restaurants. Just show your membership card in the senior club, and you're a privileged customer.

Keep Your Age Your Own Business
Red Alert! If you want your age to remain confidential between you and your banker, ask to see a sample of the free checks you'll be using as a privileged, senior customer. Some have SENIOR written on them, either in so many words or in some obvious code such as "Golden Age Account." Everyone who receives a check from you will know you're a senior citizen. The price of that "free" account may be higher than you choose to pay.

Virtually every bank offers an attractive program for seniors. The goal is to find the deal(s) that benefit you best even if it means banking in several places in person, by telephone, and online. Sorry, but some deals are available only online so you won't find telephone numbers for every listing. Senior benefits commonly offered include:

• Free checking and checks
• Fee-free bank credit cards, debit cards, and/or ATM cards/transactions
• Free or discounted safety deposit box
• Free use of the bank's copy machine
• Travel discounts and sometimes an accidental travel death insurance coverage up to $500,000
• Free travelers' checks, money orders, notary services
• Social events, free or at modest prices
• Bonus rate on CDs
• Discounts at local businesses

FANTASTIC DISCOUNTS & DEALS FOR ANYONE OVER 50!

• Free local faxes
• A special key ring that allows lost keys to be reunited with you at no charge.
• A newsy magazine or newsletter.

It can't be said too often. Read the fine print. Checks may be free only for the first year or for the first 100-250 checks. The safety deposit box may be free the first year but only discounted the next–and it's the smallest size. The bonus rate on CDs may be only 1/5th of 1%. You might do better at another bank or credit union that doesn't have a senior club. Lastly, be sure to keep your balance above the required minimum or you'll find yourself paying the same, high fees that younger depositors pay and perhaps additional fees too.

Here are some banks that pamper seniors. Note that even small, regional banks may offer online banking, so Internet-savvy seniors can shop nationwide, even worldwide, for the highest interest rates and lowest service fees. Your hometown bank may be best for some services. Call or walk in, and ask. Then try the Internet to search far and wide for the best deals. In visiting dozens of banks' websites, you'll find that few reveal senior discounts readily. You have to dig for them on the website or perhaps email the bank and ask. Sorry, but many do not have toll-free telephone numbers and some accounts are available only online.

Bank of America has free checking for people 50 and over and many more benefits. Check your local White Pages.

Bank of Lafayette is a small, Georgia family of banks that offer seniors aged 55 and better free checking if they maintain a balance that doesn't fall below $100. Other pluses include $100,000 travel accident insurance, free key return, and emergency cash advances. Tel. 706/638-2520, www.bankoflafayette.com.

Canadian Imperial Bank of Commerce has the CIBC Advantage program for people who are 60 and over.

Citizens Banks of Tennessee and Virginia have an Advantage 50 offer that includes free checking and many other privileges for people who maintain a minimum $500 balance. Get a discount on loans, safety deposit box rental, printed checks, travel and much more. Tel. 877/543-8745, www.citizensbank.com.

Coast Capital Savings is a Canadian banking group that offers senior discounts and freebies. Both Canadian and U.S. dollar accounts are available. Tel. 604/273-8138, www.coastcapitalsavings.com.

Cole Taylor Banks in the Chicago area cater to small businesspersons for both business and personal accounts. People who are 55 and over and who maintain a $250 minimum balance get free checking, four free ATM transactions monthly, bonus CD rates and much more. Ask for the New Horizons account. Tel. 773/579-2020, www.ctbnk.com.

Community Bank of Louisiana has a 55 Plus schedule of discounts and freebies for seniors plus an unusual offer. If you've been a depositor at the bank five years or more, you get "senior" privileges no matter what your age.

Farmers and Merchants Banks of Maryland have a number of senior programs including discounts, free services and social meetings. Tel. 800/695-3092, www.fmnb.com.

First Banking Centers, a Wisconsin chain, offer Gold Club membership to people aged 55 and over. With it and a combined balance (checking CDs, IRAs, etc.) that does fall below $5,000, members get a long list of benefits including many banking services such as free checking, ATM use and checks, free use of the bank's copy machine, travel discounts and much more. It's a convenience for seniors who live in Wisconsin but anyone can bank with them online. Tel. 800/456-1500, www.firstbankingcenter.com.

First Interstate Banks are found throughout Wyoming and Montana, offering people aged 50 and higher a Senior Rewards program with no-fee checking, bonus interest on CDs for terms longer than two years, and a discount on a safety deposit box. Tel. 888/752-3332, www.firstinterstatebank.com.

First National Bank, a small chain in Southwest Michigan, has a Horizons Club for people who are 50 or over and who have a minimum of $2,500 in checking or savings or at least $5,000 in CDs. The group has social functions, a no-free debit card, discounts at local merchants, and much more plus a small bonus rate for CDs. Tel. 877/273-1715, www.fnbtr.com.

First National Bank Hartford, a small family of banks in Wisconsin, invites seniors aged 50 and up to join the Prime Time Club. Maintain a balance of at least $1,500 in one or more accounts and take advantage of free, interest-bearing checking, a newsletter, travel perks, free notary services and copies, free bill-paying for some services and more. Tel. 800/945-0195, www.fnb-hartford.com.

First Ontario banks of Canada offer a senior discount and other features. For details, go to

First Source Banking centers are found in 64 locations in northern Indiana and southwestern Michigan. They offer two programs, one for people aged 50-62 and an even better deal for people aged 62 and over. Tel. 888/258-3150, www.firstsourcebanking.com.

Grange National Bank is a group serving Northeast Pennsylvania with full-service banking and many senior advantages including social programs. The Senior Saver program at $4 monthly requires no minimum balance and provides many benefits and discounts; the Senior Advantage program offers many more free services but requires a minimum balance of $2,500. Tel. 888/214-9132, www.grangebank.com.

Heritage Banks found in Washington have a Senior Advantage program that allows for free checking with no monthly fee or minimum. The program also provides free ATM transations, interest on checking balances above $500, and other features. Tel. 360/943-1500, www.heritagebank.com.

Holy Trinity Credit Union in Manitoba has a no-minimum, no-free checking service for seniors ages 60 and over. Senior services are available at two levels; other features include free traveler's checks and free bill paying. Tel. 204/949-5888, www.HolySpirit.com.

Jefferson Bank & Trust is a St. Louis-area group that offers a VIP Account to customers who are 50 and over. No minimum balance is required to get free checks. For the whole story, Tel. 314/621-0100, www.jbt-stl.com.

Kalamazoo County State Banks in Michigan invite people who are 62 and over to open a Senior Checking account that requires no minimum balance. With the deal come hotel and rental car discounts and a bonus interest rate on CDs. If you're local, contact a local branch or go to www.kscbank.com. **Pennstar Banks** throughout Pennsylvania offer people who are 55 and older a choice of three programs that offer increasing benefits according to the size of your deposit. Thanks to Gold Star Checking, Star Plus, and Gold Star Plus, seniors get additional interest for larger accounts. The simplest account offers free checking with no minimum; at the highest level, interest is paid on a no-fee checking account. Other perks include two free cashiers checks a month, travel discounts, and one free order of checks per year. Tel. 866/ 4STAR-PA, www.pennstarbank.com.

Niagara Credit Unions in Canada offer services including automatic utilities bill payment, discounted safety deposit boxes and checks, and U.S. dollar accounts for Canadians who do business south of the border. Special discounts are available to those who are 60 and over. Contact www.niagaracu.com.

Planters First banks of Georgia offer free checking and other privileges to people who are 50 and up and who maintain a balance of at least $2,500. Tel. 877/445-8814, www.plantersfirst.com.

Royal Bank of Canada offers Canadian seniors ages 60 and higher a monthly rebate on fees. Look into the deal at www.royalbank.com.

Seneca National Bank is a small bank group in South Carolina, where people who are 50 and over get two free checking accounts if they have $5,000 in savings or $10,000 in money market or other accounts. The larger the account, the larger the interest rate. Ask about Seneca Gold, www.senacanb.com.

Scotia Banks are found worldwide, so they are of special interest to Americans and Canadians who travel between the U.S. and Canada or from North America to the U.K. or Caribbean. The banks do not, however, have many traditional banking outlets in the United States. The Senior Plus account is available at age 59. Tel. 800/387-6466 in the U.S. and Canada, www.scotiabank.com.

The State Bank group is a small, Michigan chain that invites people who are 50 and over to join the Forget-Me-Not Club with its free VISA card, free local faxes, Friday night bingo, day trips, and many other benefits including a box of free checks each year. Tel. 810/629-2263; www.thestatebank.com.

Sun Trust banks are 1,800 strong in Georgia, Florida, Alabama, Tennessee, Maryland, Virginia and the District of Columbia. While the website alludes to a senior check account, follow-through was poor so it's best to make personal contact at a local branch. To find yours, tel. 800/SUNTRUST (786-8787), www.suntrust.com.

UMB Banks are found at more than 160 locations in Colorado, Kansas, Missouri, Illinois and Oklahoma. Customers aged 50 and over get a long list of advantages including a free $500,000 travel insurance policy, a discount on an auto loan, a preferred interest rate on a VISA Gold card, discounted checks, overdraft protection on some accounts, and much more. Tel. 800/821-2171, www.umb.com.

Union Bank and Trust is a small, Arkansas family that offers seniors free checking, free checks and other special treatment. For details Tel. 870/460-4600, www.unionbank.com.

U.S. Bankcorp is one of the United States' largest bank families with more than 2,100 offices nationwide and more than 4,600 ATMs, which is a plus for people on the go because fees at your own ATM are almost always less than those at other brands. Fee-free Senior Value Checking is available to people aged 50 and over. Tel. 800/US-BANKS, www.usbank.com.

Wachovia, based in Charlotte NC and one of the largest banking groups in the United States, offers no-minimum, no-fee checking for people aged 50 and better. Ask about the Fifty Plus program and the banks' many other depositor programs that can be combined into greater interest and fewer fees depending on your minimum monthly balance. Tel. 800/275-3862, www.wachovia.com.

WesBanco locations in Ohio and West Virginia invite seniors to join their Freedom 50 Club for free checking and other services. With a larger deposit, get even more advantages as a member of the Freedom 50 Gold Club. Tel. 800/328-3369, www.wesbanoc.com.

Whitney Banks are found in more than 125 locations in Louisiana, Mississippi, Texas, Alabama and the Florida Panhandle. Ask about their special savings for senior citizens, Tel. 800/681-9015, www.whitneybank.com.

3. Deals for Dining

There is a lesson here. I took Mother to lunch at the local member of an internationally-known sandwich shop chain. At the cash register, I asked quietly about the senior discount. The cashier looked at me as if I'd tried to panhandle a meal and shouted across her shoulder, "Hey Marge, do we have a senior discount?" Every eye in the restaurant turned my way as Marge shouted even more loudly to Rick across the room, who eventually bellowed the news that no, they don't have a senior discount. I felt foolish and a foot tall.

That restaurant chain is listed below because some of its franchisees do offer a senior discount and do so without bellowing the news to everyone in the place. However, my experience taught me the importance of calling ahead, unless your hide is thick as a rhino's, to avoid embarrassment at the checkout line. Even so, the person who totals your bill may not know about the discount that was promised you on the phone, resulting in humiliating dialogs like the above. Some restaurants, servers and cashiers are simply more senior-friendly than others.

Despite the occasional glitch, few senior discounts are more welcome and appealing than those found in restaurants. The day you turn 50, start watching for deals and discounts, some of them found only in fine print. While some servers will automatically knock off the discount if you have white hair, others are afraid to offer a senior discount to anyone for fear of offending someone who is young or thinks they look young. At the East Buffet in Bridgeport CT, for example, people aged 65 and older will have $1 knocked off their bill "when they ask." **The burden is on you to seek out these discounts and ask for them.**

Restaurants, like other businesses, have their own rules regarding:

•**Age.** Most restaurant discounts start at age 60 and higher, but some apply earlier. Sometimes a young cashier will simply give you the discount if you look like a senior citizen. Remember when you were 18 and thought 40-year-olds were ancient?

•**Coupons** are a popular promotional tool at many price-appeal restaurants. Usually they are good for a discount, free drink, or a buy- one-get-one-free deal. Since coupons can rarely be used in combination with the regular senior discount, do the math and use the one that is the better deal.

•**Hours.** Sometimes the senior discount is offered only during hours of the day or only during certain hours on certain days. Also, some discounts apply only to eat-in meals, not to take-out or delivery.

•**Menu.** Senior prices may apply only to a special dish or a special menu. If you're a hearty eater, you may not like the senior menu, which is down-sized. On the plus side, some restaurants offer small-portion, senior specials at all hours and they're a boon to seniors who eat lightly or are trying to.

•**Freebies.** Instead of a discount, some restaurants offer seniors a free beverage or unlimited refills on beverages.

•**Timing.** To get the discount, you may have to present a card or coupon when ordering or even when making reservations. This is often for your protection, allowing the server to guide you in choices that are allowable under the terms of the coupon and avoiding unpleasant misunderstandings when the bill comes.

•**Two For the Price of One.** Called "two-fers", these deals are a slap at widows, singles, business travelers, and anyone else who dines alone by necessity or choice. Nevertheless, they're the only break seniors can get at some places. Actually, it isn't a bad deal if you can find a friend to go with you. Or, buy yourself two dinners, one to dine in and another to go. Watch for little traps, such as a requirement to buy two beverages or the automatic addition of a 15% tip on the total of what the two meals would have cost. A similar deal is the "Buy One, Get One Half Off" deal, which amounts to a discount of up to 25% for two. The discount applies to the cheaper meal, so the actual savings could be small if you order the chopped steak and your dining partner orders filet mignon.

•**Qualification.** Be prepared to show your driver's license or other proof of age, just in case. Some restaurants require seniors to register for a discount card or a frequent-diner punch card. Every time you pay for a dinner, the card is punched. When it's full, it's good for a free meal. Some cards are free; other require a token fee. Some restaurant discounts are only offered to AARP members, so be prepared to show your membership card.

Note that not all restaurants within the same chain observe the same discounts. Don't assume that the Belt Buster Café you encounter on the road offers the same deal as the Belt Buster Café in your hometown. Even coupons can be confusing because the micro-fine print usually refers to "participating dealers" or "participating restaurants." Not every franchise owner is willing to play ball with headquarters. This is especially true of franchisees in high-rent locations such as theme parks, mall food courts, or airline terminals. Ask in advance.

Discounts, schmiscounts. The most economical way to eat at the restaurant of your choice might not be the senior discount or early bird specials but to take your grandchildren! For example, Perkins Restaurant and Bakery is a popular chain eatery where, in some cities, seniors get a15% discount on Sundays between 4 and 10pm. Since kids eat free on Tuesday 4-9pm, seniors with a gaggle of grandchildren would be better off skipping the Sunday discount. Instead, eat there on Tuesday, pay full price for your own meal, and let the children have the treats of their choice, free. At the same time, you're earning the gratitude of their harried parents, who are having a quiet dinner all to themselves at home.

Most restaurants that serve alcohol offer Happy Hour specials from, say, 4 or 5pm to 6 or 7 pm. Regardless of age, you can have a drink before dinner and still slip into the dining room in time for the Early Bird Special. At some bars, the spread of free hors d'oeuvres is so lavish, you can buy one or two drinks at the Happy Hour price and make a meal out of the canapes. While this isn't a good plan if you're driving, it starts off a nice evening in a hotel where you'll be going back to your room to order a light supper from room service.

Restaurants that serve breakfast all day can also be a bonanza to seniors who prefer a simple plate of pancakes or bacon and eggs for lunch or supper. While other diners are soldiering through salad, rolls, and heavy main dishes, you can be dusting off a delicious breakfast for a fraction of the cost of luncheon and dinner dishes. Chains that usually offer breakfast any time include Huddle House, IHOP, and Waffle House.

Getting Restaurant Discounts

Where toll-free numbers or websites were available we have listed them, but not all chains have a national contact number. Check the White or Yellow Pages to find addresses for these chain restaurants in your home town. Call ahead to ask what the discount is, at what age it applies, and how you get it. Senior discounts are rarely mentioned on websites.

Remember, the more inquiries a restaurant gets about senior discounts, the more they realize the buying power of people aged 50 and over and the more likely they are to offer a price break to them. Ask and keep asking, take your business to restaurants that care about seniors, and thank them.

Applebee's Neighborhood Grill & Bar is an international chain found at more than1,400 locations in North America and elsewhere. A sit-down restaurant in the moderate price range, the chain specializes in steaks, buttermilk shrimp, honey-grilled salmon and other tasty favorites plus bar drinks. Managers make their own decisions about senior discounts, so ask about the Golden Apple Card if you're 55 or better. It's not honored at every Applebee's and discounts differ from place to place, but it's a good deal if you hang out regularly at a local Applebee's that has a good discount. Tel. 888/ 59-APPLE, www.applebees.com.

Arby's is known for its meaty, barbecue sandwiches with basic trimmings. Buy them singly or by the bag. They travel well and are good hot or cold. Discounts vary by location, but most Arby's offer a 10% discount to people who are 55 and up.

Baker's Square Restaurant & Pies in the Chicago area take 10% off the bill if you're 60 or over. Enjoy homestyle meals or soup and a sandwich, always saving space for a slab of their famous pie.

Barnhill's buffet restaurants are found in eight states: Alabama, Arkansas, Florida, Georgia, Louisiana, Mississippi, Tennessee and Texas. They're known for southern cooking that covers football field-size buffets with fried chicken, catfish, greens, fried okra, candied yams, chicken pot pie, black-eyed peas, cornbread dressing, mashed potatoes, and other southern favorites plus rafts of fresh salads and mouthwatering desserts including cherry cobbler, pie, hot cookies, ice cream, and fat-free frozen yogurt you can trim with the toppings of your choice. Each day, a sugar-free dessert is also offered. Monday through Saturday, seniors ages 60 and better can dine for $5.19 plus tax 1-4pm. The price includes the buffet, a drink and the dessert bar but not the nightly sirloin carving station, which doesn't open until 4 p.m. For locations, go to www.barnhills.com. Added bonus: take the grandchildren, especially on Saturday when their favorite chicken nuggets, corn dogs and macaroni and cheese are on the buffet. Monday-Saturday, children ages 3-12 eat lunch for 47 cents times their age. Dinner Monday through Saturday and all day Sunday costs 52 cents times their age. Children ages 2 and under eat free. Note: we have also encountered Barnhill's where a senior discount of $.50 off the buffet applied at all times for those 60 and over. If you're in doubt, call ahead.

Bennigan's is a moderately priced, international chain known for its steaks, burgers and convivial bar. You can't count on finding senior discount here, but some outlets do offer one–if not year round, then during certain seasons. Check the White Pages and call ahead.

Bickford's Family Restaurants are found in the Northeast, especially in the Connecticut Valley, serving comfort food classics that are sure to please the whole family from seniors to the smallest grandchildren. Most locations are open around the clock and breakfast is served any time. Seniors ages 55 and better get a 25% discount every day 2-6pm. To find a Bickford's in your area, check the White or Yellow Pages or go to www.bickfordsrestaurants.com.

Black-Eyed Pea is a Southern chain of sit-down restaurants offering trendy versions of traditional Southern fare. People of any age can order from a special menu that provides smaller portions at smaller prices. Check the local phone book to see if your area has a Black-Eyed Pea.

Burger King fast food restaurants usually offer seniors free coffee or tea with a food order, but franchisees are independent and set their own policies. Found worldwide, these restaurants are favored for burgers and fries, frosty drinks and quick service inside or drive-through.

Captain D's seafood restaurants don't all participate in a senior discount program, but call ahead to see if your local Captain has Senior Citizen Day on Wednesday, with a 10% discount.

Carl's Jr. is a fast food chain in the Western states and Hawaii (almost 700 locations in California alone) that usually offers 10% off to people 55 and older. Discounts could vary with location. They're famous for big, juicy, two-fisted sandwiches, their "$6 burger" for $3.95 and for their motto, "If it doesn't get all over the place, it doesn't belong in your face®." Find restaurant locations by going to www.carlsjr.com.

Casinos that have a restaurant usually offer a 10% senior discount on meals or $1 off the buffet. Even if you are not a gambler, check out dining at casinos, dog tracks, jai alai, and horse tracks.

Carrows Restaurants offer full-service, sit-down, family dining at 141 places in Western States. They're a good place to go with the grandchildren because special menus with special prices are available for children and for seniors aged 55 and over. Tel. 877/225-4161, www.carrows.com.

Chili's Grill & Bar restaurants are found nationwide, specializing in steaks, burgers, sandwiches, and cold beer as well as bar drinks. Not all restaurants participate in the senior discount program, but those that do offer a 10% discount to people aged 55 and over.

Church's Chicken is a national chain known for its golden, crusty chicken and all the trimmings. If you're 65 or older, ask for the 10% discount.

Cracker Barrel restaurants nationwide are eternal favorites for their home-spun menu and big gift shops that are a destination in themselves. Usually they're found along interstates so, if you're on a long journey, ask about their audio tape rental program. Pick up a book on tape at one Cracker Barrel; turn it in at another. The restaurants are known for their big portions, but seniors ages 50 and over are welcome to order off the children's menu, where you can get smaller portions at smaller prices.

D and W is a downstate Illinois chain of family restaurants where seniors are invited to order smaller, "senior" plates at $1.50 off full price.

Dairy Queen, known popularly as DQ, serves much more than frozen custard: hot dogs, burgers, shakes, sundaes, and much more. At least some of them offer a senior discount of 10% but ages and rules vary. Phone ahead. Check the White Pages.

Dennys is a widespread chain of moderately-priced, sit-down restaurants specializing in hearty breakfasts, old-fashioned main dishes, hot and cold sandwiches, salads and excellent soups. The senior citizen menu, available any time, offers a good selection of foods in smaller portions at smaller prices.

Domino's Pizza shops are found throughout North America and many offer a 20% discount to people who are 62 and older. Call to ask about the deal, then comparison-shop because the chain publishes a lot of coupons that may be a better deal than the senior discount. You have to choose one or the other; both discounts can't be used in combination. If you're ordering for delivery, ask whether the senior discount applies to that too.

Fazoli's fast food restaurants are found nationwide. Stop in for a big, juicy, hot sub or a special pizza or pasta meal at affordable prices. Participating locations offer a 10% senior discount, usually for those aged 60 and up, but it's wise to call ahead and get the full story. See the White Pages.

Furr's Family Dining, a chain found in Texas and the South, offers 10% off its all-you-can-eat feasts for people ages 55 and over. Watch for it.

Golden Corral is a national chain of family steak houses with bodacious buffets that are a favorite with seniors. Order a steak cooked to order if you like, and complete your menu with mountains of salad, chicken, roast beef, pork, mashed potatoes, vegetables, fruit and a choice of desserts. They're all a little different, some better than others. The regular price is $9-$10 for the works; participating franchisees in Central Florida offer seniors a $4.99 (plus tax) buffet Monday through Friday 1-3 pm. Call each restaurant ahead to ask about their senior deals, which vary around the country.

Grandy's is a small, Texas group of family restaurants where seniors ages 65 and over can ask for the 10% discount. Check local White or Yellow Pages to see if there is a Grandy's near you.

Hardee's hamburger restaurants cook up a juicy, flame-boiled burger like no other. If you're 55 or better, ask for the 10% discount.

Hoss's Family Steak and Sea House restaurants are found at dozens of locations in the Mid-Atlantic states including Pennsylvania and Delaware as well as in Virginia and West Virginia. They're known for a sumptuous soup and salad bar with help-yourself sundaes for dessert. Add a sandwich to the salad bar for another buck. The list of Midwestern steaks is as big as Texas, everything from petite filets to 16-ounce sirloins, all cooked to order and available with a big side dish of sauteed mushrooms. Then there are chicken dishes, raft-size seafood platters, and combination platters. Order any menu item in the full or light plate version. Seniors ages 60 and over get a 10% discount any time and a 25% price cut Monday-Saturday 1:30-4pm only. Check the White or Yellow Pages to see if there's a Hoss's in your city or go to www.hoss.com.

Huddle House restaurants are always open, little havens of warmth and diner fare served fast and at affordable prices for insomniacs who want supper at midnight, fishermen who want breakfast at 5 a.m., workers who want a big feed when the noon whistle blows, and everyone in between. You'll find them along major highways and interstates, www.huddlehouse.com. Look for the "lite" dishes, which are ideal for seniors with small appetites. There is no special, senior discount.

IHOP used to be known as the International House of Pancakes, but it serves much more than pancakes. Found throughout North America and elsewhere, most are open around the clock. Have blueberry pancakes for breakfast, a big sandwich for lunch and a meat-and-potatoes dinner. The senior menu offers smaller portions. Seniors ages 55 and better get a 10% discount. Check your local phone book.

Jack in the Box fast-food restaurants nationwide are popular for their hamburgers, hot and cold sandwiches, icy drinks, and drive-through convenience. If you're 55 or better, they'll cut the price of your beverage by 50 cents.

Just Desserts is a chain we've seen only in the San Francisco area, but there may be one near you. The discount is 10% for those aged 55 and better.

Kenny Rogers Roasters are found in major population centers, offering chicken and all the trimmings to eat in or take away. A 10% discount goes to those who are 65 or older.

Krispy Kreme donuts are taking the world by storm so you're likely to find them at home and everywhere you travel. The senior discount starts at age 50 and saves 10%.

Le Peep restaurants are usually in downtown locations, offering breakfast and lunch delicacies. Senior discounts vary, but are usually 10% for people 55 and older.

Luby's Cafeterias are a widespread American chain known for generous portions of lusty, comfort foods. Choose your own main dish and just the right trimmings, followed by desserts to die for. Most Luby's have a senior discount, but ages and deals vary. Usually the discount starts at age 50 and amounts to 10% on certain nights, but other Luby's offer seniors a discount only on the LuAnn special. Check local White or Yellow Pages, then call ahead.

Long John Silver fast food fish houses usually offer seniors who are 55 and over a 10% discount or a discounted beverage. Ask as you go. Watch too for coupons, which may offer a better deal than the senior discount and cannot be used with it.

McDonald's don't have a stated, world-wide senior discount policy because 85% of the restaurants are individually owned and allowed to set their own policies. The only way to know is to ask as you go. You'll win some, lose some. For general inquiries, complaints, or to find a McDonald's new you, Tel. 800/244-6227, www.McDonalds.com.

Mrs. Field's Cookies are usually found in mall locations nationwide selling cookies and beverages. As a snack these cookies are irresistible; a dozen cookies or one supercookie also make gifts suitable for any occasion. Seniors ages 60 and higher get a 10% discount.

Miami Subs Grill is a widespread Eastern chain we've seen in the Northeast and in Florida including one located in a rest plaza on the Florida Turnpike. They specialize in hot and cold sandwiches, colorful dinner plates, salads and smoothies, all with a wholesome spin. If you're 65 or better, ask about the 10% discount.

New York, New York is a wonderful city for dining out, especially when you take advantage of price breaks. Send $1 and a self-addressed 9 X 12-inch envelope to NYC Department of Consumer Affairs, Senior Dining Guide, 42 Broadway, New York NY 10004. More than 300 New York restaurants offer either early bird specials or senior discounts, which are described in this guide.

Old Country Buffet and **HomeTown Café** restaurants sell a Senior Club Card for $1 a year to anyone over 60. With it, diners get a discount of 6-12% plus entry in a weekly drawing for a free meal. The chain is nationwide but names vary, so look for the words HomeTown or Old Country in the restaurant name.

Perkins Restaurants are a popular, national chain known for hearty main dishes, hot and cold sandwich plates, homemade soups, and people-pleasing pies, all in a moderate price range. Many now service alcohol. Senior discount policies vary and usually apply only to certain hours on some days. Call ahead. The company often advertises buy-one, get-one specials that are good any time, at any age. They may be a better buy than the senior discount, so do the math.

Pasta Connection is a small but growing chain of fast food restaurants with an Italian accent. Locations are widespread from Washington and the Dakotas to the Northeast, Kentucky and Tennessee. Check local White or Yellow Pages or do a search online for Pasta Connection to see if there is one in your area. Discounts vary by location but are usually 10% for people aged 55 and better.

Piccadilly Cafeterias, sometimes free-standing and also found in malls, spread an irresistible buffet of old-fashioned favorites including their famous Blue Plate Specials and homemade pies. Monday through Wednesday between 2 and 5pm, people age 60 and over get a 10% discount.

Pizza Hut offers a 15% discount to persons who are 62 and over. The chain runs a lot of coupons, however, so watch for them and compare. They may be a better deal than the senior discount and cannot be combined with it.

Popeye Chicken & Biscuits is a national, fast food chain with easy, drive-through takeout popular for crispy, tangy, fried chicken and old-fashioned biscuits. If you're aged 60 or better, ask for the 10% discount.

Ryan's Steak House is a popular, national chain that features cooked-to-order steaks plus an enormous choice from a buffet filled with seas of side dishes. Discounts may vary locally, but some outlets offer a senior discount of 10% every day. Others offer the discount only at certain times or are on certain days.

Shoney's fast food outlets are favorites of those who love a good hamburger or sandwich with fries and a soft drink or hot coffee. Most Shoney's offer people who are 55 or over either a $.50 discount off a main dish or $1 off the salad bar or buffet. Some offer a straight, 10% discount. Call ahead.

Steak and Ale restaurants have hearty, meat-and-potatoes meals, excellent salads, and a convivial, pub-like, bar atmosphere. The chain doesn't have a standard senior discount policy, but call ahead and ask because seasonal promotions are often in place.

Subway restaurants are independently owned and headquarters does not know which franchisees offer a senior discount. However, it's at their discretion and may occur here and there, so ask as you go. The chain is a big advertiser, so watch for coupons. For general comments on Subway, Tel. 800/888-4848, www.subway.com.

TCBY is found in mall food courts, at airports and in freestanding locations, and not all will give seniors a discount but many will knock off 10% if you're 55 or more. The name stands for The Country's Best Yogurt, which we don't dispute. Fat-free, sugar-free selections offered at some locations are guilt free and delicious.

TGI Friday's is one of those relaxed, after-work places where people gather for a drink, good conversation, and hearty meals centered around meat and potatoes or perhaps a mile-high burger with all the trimmings. At participating restaurants, seniors aged 63 and over get a 50% discount on a cup of coffee.

T.J. Cinnamon's is a Midwestern chain of eateries that are popular for breakfast, coffee break, lunch and snacks. A 10% discount is yours if you are 55 or better.

Taco Bell restaurants are individually owned, with no senior discount policy that applies chain-wide. Some offer no discount; others may discount the entire meal, the beverage, or offer free refills on drinks. Ask. For general comments, complaints or to locate a Taco Bell near you, Tel. 800/TACO-BELL, www.TacoBell.com.

Waffle House restaurants now number more than 1,300 in 24 states in handy, highway locations. They're famous for waffles, of course, but you'll find three meals a day here around the clock. The senior menu shows reduced portions at reduced prices. Tel. 877/992-3353, www.wafflehouse.com.

---

iDine

Early bird specials are almost synonymous with senior citizen, but some seniors prefer to dine later. One way to beat high prices is to join a group such as www.iDine.com. For $49 per person per year, get up to 20% off restaurant meals, hotels and other services including, in some cases, frequent flyer miles. At press time, more than 8,000 sites participate in the iDine plan, so check out the website to see if enough discounts are available in your area to make it worth the yearly payout. Similar local deals may also be available through newspapers, lifestyle magazines, the Chamber of Commerce or even through organizations that sell discount booklets as a fund raiser. You buy the book of coupons, which are good for a straight discount (which is better for those who dine alone), or a two-fer deal such as buy one, get one free, or buy one and get the second half off. Make sure you understand the rules, and will dine out enough to recoup the high price of the coupon book.

Wendy's is beloved for its two-fisted hamburgers as well as salads, hot sandwiches, baked potatoes with all the trimmings, fries, desserts and beverages. Individual franchisees may discount your drink or meal, depending on the restaurant. If you're 55 or better, ask what price break is available. For general information, complaints and comments, Tel. 800/443-7266, www.wendys.com.

Western Sizzlin' is a chain of steak houses in the economy price range, favored for its substantial cuts of meat, salad bar, and a choice of potato. Not every location participates, but many offer a 10% discount to those who are 55 and over. Call ahead.

Quiznos Classic Subs are a different twist on a favorite theme: big submarine sandwiches that are heated to a toasty, melty, delicious meal. If you're 60 or better, call ahead to ask about the 10% discount that some Quinznos offer.

4. Flying High for Low Fares
Planes, Trains, Buses, Car and RV Rentals

Red Alert! If a travel professional is making arrangements for you, make sure he or she knows your age and takes advantage of all price breaks that are available to you. In a complicated air-sea-land-meals-guides-car rental package, only some segments may be eligible for a senior discount, which your travel agent can assure for you. If you're over 70, ask your travel agent to make sure a car rental is available where you're going. In some countries, rental agencies have age limits.

AIRFARES
Troubled airlines have been shedding senior discounts quicker than they can say, "Coffee, tea, or milk." Still, it's worth asking, asking, asking. Although most discounts don't kick in until you're 62, start asking as soon as you hit the double nickel.

Note that senior discounts almost always apply only to published fares. Always shop and compare, especially if you can navigate your way around discount travel websites, because other fares such as last-minute travel, special promotions, and package deals with cruises or resorts are usually better than senior fares.

While you're on Hold waiting to talk to a ticket agent, airlines tell you that the best prices are probably available at their website. This is rarely true when it comes to seniors. By all means, check websites but it usually takes voice contact to score the best senior price. Senior rates are not mentioned on most airline websites.

Senior fares, where available, are a bonanza for 55-plus people who are still in the work force and who travel on business. When you're fully in the work force, you may not think of yourself as a senior citizen even when you reach

62, 65, and even higher. Some of industrys' most influential, active and productive people are seniors who could be traveling at senior rates. If you're a frequent traveler, consider subscribing to Best Fares magazine. It costs $59.95 a year, which includes membership, a bimonthly magazine, and a long list of perks. The magazine has a special section devoted just to senior discounts. Tel. 800/880-1234, www.bestfares.com.

In comparison shopping for airfare, note whether younger companions can travel at the senior citizen price. Often, they can. Keep asking, however, whether a better deal is available because some airlines, at some times, offer companions-fly-free deals that are a better deal than two senior fares. If you're traveling with young grandchildren, ask about children's rates, which may be cheaper than the senior companion fare. If your companion(s) are ages 18-22, they may get a better price with a student or "X" fare. Since senior discounts are rarely mentioned on airline websites, it's best to compare fares both at the website and with a human operator.

Aerolineas Argentinas offers a 10 percent discount to seniors ages 60 and over but only for flights that originate in the United States. Tel. 800/333-0276, www.aerolinasargentinas.com.

AeroMexico will take 10 percent off if you're 62 or over and the flight originates in the United States. Tel. 237-6639, www.aeromexico.com.

Air Canada takes 10 percent off its published fares unless otherwise noted in an advertisement or web posting. If you're 60 or older, or will be by the time you take the trip, ask for the discount. At check-in you'll need a photo

---

About Airline Discounts for Seniors

Airlines being airlines, there is enough fine print in every deal to stretch from here to JFK and back. Get out the magnifying glass so you won't be torpedoed by blackout dates, re-booking fees, minimum stay, cancellation fees, fare zones, passenger facility charges and other taxes and fees, and city or state exceptions. One more wrinkle: for security reasons, the name on your ticket must match exactly the name on your passport, driver's license or other photo I.D. If it does not, you may have to pay $100 for a re-issued ticket.

ID with your birth date. Discounts to places other than North America or the United Kingdom may be different, or unavailable. Tel. 888/247-2262, www.aircanada.ca.

Air France will take 10 percent off for seniors ages 62 and older if the flight originates in the United States. The discount follows you throughout the trip including connecting flights. Tel. 800/237-2747, www.airfrance.com.

Air Jamaica discounts flights between the United States and Jamaica for people ages 60 and up. Tel. 800/523-5585, www.airjamaica.com.

Alaska Airlines gives a 10 percent discount to people aged 62 and higher. Tel. 800/252-7522, www.alaskaair.com.

Alitalia flights that originate in the United States are priced 10 percent less for seniors ages 62 and better. Tel. 800/223-5730. www.alitaliausa.com.

America West America West gives a 10 percent discount to those who are 62 and up sells senior coupons, which are almost always an excellent value, especially for those who fly long distances several times a year. For $596, persons aged 62 and higher can buy four coupons good for four one-way flights for themselves and for accompanying grandchildren ages 2-11. Some blackout dates apply, a 14-day advance purchase is required, and coupons are good for up to a year. Other rules apply regarding standby, re-issue, and changing tickets. Ask too about senior discounts off published fares. Tel. 800/235-9292, www.americawest.com.

American Airlines got a lot of media attention when it was one of the first airlines to bring its senior discount to a bumpy halt. Times are too turbulent to predict what discounts are in place at any moment. If you can find a deal at all, advance-purchase requirements are longer, minimum stays shorter, fares higher . For the latest, Tel. 800/433-7300, www.aa.com.

Austrian Airlines discounts flights 10 percent for people age 62 and higher. Flights must originate in the United States. Tel. 800/843-0002, www.austrianair.com.

ATA offers a 10 percent discount to people who are 62 or older. Tel. 800/435-9282.

British Airways discounts its fares 10 percent for seniors and for companions or spouses of any age. Tel. 800/247-9297, www.britishairways.com.

British Midland offers a 10 percent discount on all its routes as long as the trip originates in the United States and the traveler is aged 60 or more. Tel. 800/788-0555, www.britishmidland.com.

BWIA will take you to the West Indies at a 10 percent discount if you're 62 or better. Ask about packages that include airfare, lodgings, airport transfers and many other features. Tel. 800/538-2942, www.bwia.com.

Cayman Airways discounts tickets 10 percent for people who have reached age 62. Tel./ 800/422-9626, www.caymanair.com.

Cathay Pacific offers a senior fare on some routes, some times. Tel. 800/233-2742, www.CathayPacific.com

El-Al discounts fares only for travel between New York and Israel, but you may make one stopover in each direction. A 15 percent discount applies to people over 60 and any companion or spouse who is 55 or older. Tel. 800/223-6700, www.elal.com.

Finnair will take off 10 percent for your flight originating in the United States and an even larger discount for flights within Finland if you're aged 62. Tel. 800/950-5000, www.finnair.com.

Frontier will take 10 percent off the price of a ticket if you're 62 or older. Tel. 800/432-1359, www.flyfrontier.com.

Hawaiian Air starts its discounts at age 60, and takes off 10 percent. Tel. 800/367-5320, www.hawaiianair.com.

Iberia Airlines gives a 10 percent discount when you reach 62. Tel. 800/772-4642, www.iberia.com.

Legacy Air and **Empire One** are strongest in New York State but offer connections throughout the world. Ask for Golden Wings rates if you're 55 and you'll save 15 percent. Generous discounts also apply to students and military personnel. Tel. 866/212-LEGACY, www.flylegacy.com.

Lufthansa's senior discounts start at age 60. Tel. 800/399-5838, www.lufthansa.com.

Martinair serves Holland, the Dutch West Indies and other destinations for 10 percent off if you're 62. Tel. 800/627-8462, www.martinair.com.

Mexicana's 10 percent discounts start at age 62. Tel. 800/531-7921, www.mexicana.com.

Midwest Express gives a 10 percent discount to people who are aged 55 or better. Underage spouses and companions can't piggyback on the senior's discount. Tel. 800/452-2022, www.midwestexpress.com.

National Airlines will give a 10 percent discount to those who are 65 or older. Tel. 888/757-5387, www.nationalairlines.com.

Olympic Airways' 10 percent discount applies for flights originating in the U.S. if you're 62; flights within Greece carry a 20 percent discount for those 60 and over. Tel. 800/223-1226, www.olympicair.com.

South African Airways does not offer a senior discount at this writing. To check current deals, Tel. 800/722-9675, www.saa.co.za.

Southwest Airlines became successful by thinking outside the box, so their senior deal is different from the others. It's available only by phone, and only to people 65 and older, but fares are unrestricted. At press time, the most any senior pays is $129 each way and the fare is refundable or changeable. First, check the website, www.southwest.com, to see what fares are available for the route and dates you want. Then Tel. 800/435-9792 to get the lowest senior fare.

Spanair, the Spanish airline, offers a 10 percent discount at 62. Tel. 888/545-5757, www.spanair.com.

TAP Air Portugal's discount starts at age 62 and applies only to flights that originate in the United States. Tel. 800/221-7370, www.TAPair.com.

United Airlines is another very troubled carrier at press time, but it is expected to survive. Check into its Silver Wings program. Fares are as low as $124 round-trip (within Zone A only; fares go up with distance) when you buy four certificates in advance. If you're age 62 or higher, you can buy additional sets of certificates for as little as $25. A life membership in United's Silver Wings costs $225 and buys a shipload of benefits including bonus miles as well as discounts on lodgings (up to 50% off rack rate at participating Hiltons, Sheratons and Westins), rental cars, and cruises. A two-year membership costs $75. Call 800-720-1765 or go to www.silverwingsplus.com.

USAirways discontinued its traditional senior discount but still gives an AARP discount. Tel. 800/866-2277, have your AARP membership number at hand, and ask for the AARP Savers fare for your destination and travel dates.

Virgin Atlantic starts its discounts at age 60, when a 10 percent discount applies to flights that originate in the United States. Tel. 800/862-8621, www.virginatlantic.com.

Bargain Flights Hotline!

If you're not picky about dates and destinations, you can book a round trip to the Caribbean or Europe for bargain rates with www.airtech.com or Tel. 212/219-7000. Give them a four-day window and they'll find the best rate available to a variety of destinations.

THE SMART SENIOR...

•Checks in within the prescribed time limit. Allow plenty of time for the curbside luggage line or check-in line, as well as long screening lines. If you don't get to the gate in time (10-30 minutes before departure, depending on the airline) you could lose your seat even if you have already checked in and have a boarding pass. In this case, your baggage will be found and off-loaded. Since September 11, 2001, flying is changed forever. If you miss your flight because of delays at Security, you're out of luck. It's your responsibility to get to the airport well in advance.

•Understands that not all airlines have ticketing arrangements with each other. If you fly one airline from Point A to Point B, where you'll connect for a flight from Point C to Point D, and the flight is late, you will be listed as a no-show unless both airlines are in on your arrangements. It can save a lot, especially when you're booking online, to book legs separately, but be aware of pitfalls that can be very costly.

•Realizes that kindness counts. Remember the little old lady in Arthur Hailey's book Airport, who flew everywhere free just by pretending to be sweetly addled? You can be an old crab and demand your rights, but you will catch more flies with honey than vinegar. I once praised the coffee aboard a Puerto Rico-bound flight. A steward beamed as he told me that they carry a special blend on this run because Puerto Ricans love good coffee, and he slipped me a half-pound package of it to take home! These are difficult times for all air travelers, screeners and airline personnel. Chill.

•Checks into little-known bereavement fares when a last-minute booking is necessary because of illness, death or other family emergencies. Each airline has its own, complex policy based on (1) the nature of the emergency and (2) how closely you are related to the patient, deceased or victim. Some airlines have a big heart when it comes to such trips, knocking off as much as 50 percent of the fare. You may have to pay full fare up front, then file for the discount later after getting a copy of the death certificate or other substantiation. If you're Internet-savvy and have time, check into last-minute fares at airline websites and at travel websites such as orbitz.com, lastminutefares,com and site59.com. Without time or a computer in an emergency, call airlines and ask about the bereavement fare.

BUS TRAVEL
Virtually all **local bus, subway and transit lines** offer senior discounts that vary in percentage, rules and age. Start looking for them in your hometown when you reach 55. Most kick in at age 62 or higher and you may need to get special photo ID or buy a pass by the week or month. When traveling, ask as you go. In some cases, you simply show proof of age as you board. In others, discounts are aimed more at locals and are not worth the hassle for the visitor.

Greyhound offers Senior Club membership for $5 a year to anyone aged 62 and over. Use your card to get 10% off unrestricted Greyhound passenger fares and meals in Greyhound-owned and operated restaurants, and 25 percent off Greyhound Package Express shipments. Tel. 800/229-9424, www.greyhound.com.

Grand Canyon Rail Tours takes passengers into the Grand Canyon. Seniors ages 62 and over don't have to pay the national park entrance fee, even if they do not hold a Golden Age Passport. Tel. 800/843-8724, www.thetrain.com.

Gray Line bus tours by the day and half day in the United States, Canada and Mexico are discounted 10 percent for AARP members. No matter how sophisticated a traveler you are, we recommend that a visit to a new city always be started with a bus tour. It's carefree and fun, and makes you a safer driver when you hit the bricks on your own.

TRAIN TRAVEL
Amtrak generally offers a discount of 15 percent to seniors aged 62 and over. Tel. 800/USA-RAIL, www.amtrak.com.

BritRail senior discounts start at age 60. Ask about passes, which may be a better deal if you're hitting a lot of stops in a short period. Tel. 888/274-8724, www.britrail.com

Rail Europe is the home of the famous Eurail Pass, which most North American travelers first discovered in their college days. A senior discount doesn't apply to the passes, but you can get a discount by traveling with another person. The Saver deal applies to two or more persons; a group deal may be available for six or more. Railroads in France offer a discount to people aged 60 and over; Germany's Deutsche Bahn offers the Saver pass for two, but does not give a senior discount. Tel. 888/382-7245 in the U.S. and 800/361-7245 from Canada, www.raileurope.com.

RENTAL CAR WRINKLES
Rental car companies aren't as falling-over-over-themselves eager to court seniors as are banks, hair salons, department stores, hotels and restaurants. In fact, your age can be a downright problem if you're over 75 or 80. In countries other than the United States, there may be an upper age limit on

car rental. If you are age 70 or more and are reserving a car overseas, ask to be sure.

A Smart Senior Knows That....

•Weekly car rentals aren't always cheaper than paying by the day when you need a car for only four or five days. Rates also vary according to the city and season. Ask about weekend or weekdays specials.

•Unlimited mileage has a price. When you need a car just to go short distances (such as driving just from the airport to a motel to the church while attending a family wedding), ask if you can have a lower rate for accepting a lower mileage limit. It may be available. .

•Unless you're arriving first thing in the morning, don't reserve the largest car. There is a good chance you can get upgraded when checking in. If you're willing to take the gamble, reserve the smallest car in the cheapest category. A free upgrade may be automatic or you may have to request it. Upgrading may be easier if you have certain memberships, are a frequent flyer, or have a platinum credit card.

Advantage Rent-A-Car gives a five percent discount to members of AARP or AAA. Ask for it when reserving your car. Tel. 800/775-5500, www.arac.com.

Alamo has a special rate for AARP members, but details are subject to change. Call ahead, Tel. 800/462-5266, www.alamo.com.

Avis discounts for AARP members age 50 and higher are 5 to 25 percent depending on the date, place and model. If you're not an AARP member ask what other senior discounts are available. Tel. 800/331-1212, www.avis.com.

Hertz gives AARP members ages 50 and over a discount of 5-25 percent depending on the date and model. If you're not an AARP member ask what other senior discounts are available. Tel. 800/654-3131, www.hertz.com.

National offers 5 to 20% off their regular rental rate for people over 55 and to AARP members ages 50 and up. Tel. 800/328-4567, www.national.com For international rentals, Tel. 800/ 227-3876.

If you need a car just for local driving, check your Yellow Pages. Local, non-chain rental agencies in your city may have better deals that can be found through national numbers and websites.

RENT AN RV FOR PEANUTS

El Monte RV is a nationwide RV rental fleet that needs frequent repositioning, so rentals are offered at giveaway prices for those who are willing to travel when and where the RV is needed. The company's needs change constantly according to where demand is greatest, so the deal is best for seniors who are spontaneous and flexible. There are predictable migrations between north and south spring and fall, but a great many other variations are dictated by, say, a big sports event, a festival, or a demand for trips to Walt Disney World when school lets out.

You might, for example, go from Los Angeles to Dallas in a 22-foot, Class C motorhome for $151 including 1,500 free miles and a week of RV living. Additional costs include fuel, nightly campsites, a California license fee of $14 and a $20 RV starter kit. You'll also have to get to Los Angeles or wherever the RV is located in the beginning, and back home from Dallas, or wherever you have agreed to return the RV.

The company has 1,800 rental units at more than 30 locales in the United States and Canada. El Monte RV, 12818 Firestone Boulevard, Sante Fe Springs CA 90670. Tel. 800/337-2141, elmonterv.com.

5. Oceans of Savings: Cruises

The cruise industry is doing cartwheels, shouting from the treetops, and turning itself inside out to attract younger passengers, but the truth is that your fellow passengers on most ships most of the time, will be people over 50. At age 50 and beyond, people are more likely to have leisure time and leisure dollars, and are less likely to spend them climbing mountains or squirming through an unexplored cave. It's often said that the longer the cruise, the older the passengers. The good news is that seniors, as the bread and butter of the cruise industry, are courted and catered to in many ways. A shipbuilding boom was already underway before September 11, 2001, and over-capacity soared while rates plunged. Cruising remains a buyers' market.

The bad news is that you, as a person aged 50 or better, are already a captive audience. Many cruise lines give little or no discount to seniors. If they did, hardly anyone on board would be paying full price. Here are a few lines that do give a price break to seniors. It's best to book through your travel agent or the toll-free number. Senior discounts are almost never mentioned on websites.

Alaska Glacier Bay Cruises offer various discounts on cruises and perhaps even airfare for those 62 and over. Tel. 800/451-5952, www.glacierbaytours.com.

B&V Waterways takes 5% off the cost of a cruise for AARP members. Your floating hotel will be a beamy, comfortable barge that sails the rivers and canals of Europe, never out of sight of land and never in rough waters that make you seasick. Tel. 800/546-4777 or 800/999-3636,www.ewaterways.com or bvassociates.com.

Carnival Cruise Lines give AARP members a discount of $25-$200. You must show your membership card. Join a nice mix of ages for the cruise of a lifetime. Tel. 800/327-9501, www.carnival.com.

Celebrity Cruises may have seasonal promotions for people 55 and over. Tel. 800/437-3111, www.celebritycruises.com.

Clipper Cruises specialize in small ships that can get into small ports of call in North America and abroad. Telephone to see if they're offering any senior promotions for the time and place you want to cruise. Tel. 800/325-0010, www.clippercruises.com.

Cruise West is a small-ship cruise line known for its cruises of Alaska, the Inside Passage, and the Pacific Northwest in summer and the Sea of Cortez and Central America in winter. Scenery is breathtaking ashore and afloat, meals are varied and sumptuous, and cabins have ample space and en suite baths. The seven ships carry only 70-114 passengers, so you won't stand in long lines at buffets or the gangplank. One price pays for almost everything including one shore excursion in each port. Moreover, safety standards are high to meet those of the U.S. Coast Guard; crews work under U.S. wage and labor laws. Foreign flag ships may not offer these high standards.

In partnership with AARP, the line offers senior discounts and specials such as a shipboard credit that is tied to the length of the cruise. Special programs are posted regularly; a typical AARP deal offers a shipboard credit of $200 per person on a cruise 10 nights or longer; $50 on four- and six-night cruises and $25 on three-night sailings. Since AARP membership is available to people ages 50 and better and to spouses of any age, this deal is a particular bonanza for younger couples.

While senior discounts apply only to AARP members, ask about other specials that are not age-based and are available to everyone. They include early booking discounts and free or reduced air fare on some itineraries. The line also has a generous single supplement policy on all ships to all destinations. Offer to share a cabin with another single traveler and, if one can't be found, you get the cabin to yourself, paying only the single, per-person fare based on double occupancy. Tel. 800/888-9378, www.cruisewest.com.

Costa Cruise Lines specialize in Italian style and hospitality, especially when it comes to families cruising together. Join the Italian street festival to play bocce ball, learn to dance the tarantella, wear a toga, and feast on fine Italian cuisine, all the while cruising the eastern or western Caribbean. It's the perfect way to travel as a family yet still have plenty of options in activities, food and bedtimes for everyone in every generation. In a recent deal, children ages 17 and younger are offered free cruising with two paying adults using the discounted Andiamo Advance Purchase rates starting at $499 per person, while seniors in the same party pay as little as $399 per person, double occupancy. Different promotions apply at different times of the year. Senior discounts, where available, apply at ages 60 and higher. See your travel agent or Tel. 800-33-COSTA, www.costacruises.com.

Disney Cruise Line has a lower median age than many other lines, but everyone from toddlers and honeymooners to octogenarians loves these luxury liners. Go as a couple for a romantic getaway or take the grandchildren on a cruise they'll never forget. Children's programs are the best in the industry, insuring a great time for the kids and plenty of free time for Gram and Gramps. The line has occasional promotions and specials for seniors. Tel. 800/951-3532, www.disneycruises.com.

Fred Olsen Cruise Lines sail worldwide including Canada, the Caribbean, the British Isles and Europe in small ships holding 412-727 passengers. While discounts aren't age-specific, anyone who books six months in advance gets a 30 % discount and last-minute bookings are discounted as much as 40 %. Every cruise has gentleman hosts aboard, which is good news for single women who love to dance. Your fellow passengers will be mostly ages 60 and up, so you'll find like-minded folks if you want to play bridge, bocce ball or the game the British call quoits and Americans call ring toss. The line also features golf packages with individual PGA instruction, onboard lectures and practice areas, and golf ashore at hand-picked courses. Tel. 800/346-0602, www.fredolsencruises.co.uk.

French Country Waterways Ltd. is a fleet of floating country inns, cozy and quaint, on the canals and rivers of France. We can't think of a more romantic way to cruise or a more "insider" way to explore the French countryside. Glide tree-lined canals past miles of fields filled with lavender or bright yellow canola. Stop along the way at world-famous restaurants. See medieval towns, ancient cathedrals and stately chateaux where you're treated to a private wine tasting. Float over French vineyards and chateaux in a hot air balloon. The "hotel barges" carry only 12-18 pampered guests, who get personalized service ashore and afloat, gourmet meals with wine and artisanal cheeses, and bicycles to ride along canal towpaths. Discounts match the number of the anniversary you're celebrating. Take off 5 % for your fifth and so on, up to a 60 % discount for your 60th. If you want to celebrate with friends, charter an entire boat for six to 18 guests. Book early to get the dates you want. Tel. 800/222-1236 in the U.S. and Canada and 781/934-2454 in Massachusetts, www.fcwl.com.

Golden Sun Cruise Lines gives a discount of 10-15% to seniors who book early. Tel. 877/244-8004, www.goldsuncruises.com.

Norwegian Coastal Voyage is a favorite with seniors for many reasons. For one, millions of Americans of Norwegian descent long to return to the country they heard about from their grandparents. For another, this isn't a "love boat" experience but a real coastal steamer that delivers the mail and cargo, cute kids who are on a field trip to the next fjord, and ordinary Norwegians on their way home to a remote village. Scenery is stunning, and cruising is the best way to see it. The line has a dozen ships, hundreds of cabins in all sizes and styles (including balcony suites) and makes 34 ports of call above and below the Arctic Circle.

Seniors ages 67 and better get a discount of about $20 per person per day on sailings between September 1 and April 30. That's off season, when weather can be chilly, but it's also when aurora borealis is best. If you're single, there's more good news. This is one of the few cruise lines that has single cabins at single prices. Tel. 800/323-7436, www.costalvoyage.com.

Peter Deilmann Cruises offer comforts that appeal to seniors while sparing them the huge crowds found on large cruiser liners. Since you're never out of sight of land, or in waters that make you feel whoopsy, these are cruises for people who think they don't like cruising. Cabins are spacious and have en suite baths; many have a private balcony. Meals are lavish. Dockings are frequent, and you have the choice of joining an English-speaking, guided group or exploring on your own.

Ships with only 48-100 cabins sail the Rhone, Danube and other European rivers, stopping at historic points. Shore excursions can be bought as a package, or you can buy a package that includes the cruise, shore excursions, first class hotel stays with breakfast, transfers, and city sightseeing. Ask about reduced rate packages. For example, the luxury liner MS Deutschland offers free or very low-cost air to U.S. travelers and 50% discount on pre-purchased shore excursion packages on Baltic, Mediterranean and worldwide cruises. Tel. 800/348-8287, www.deilmann-cruises.com.

Renaissance Cruises offers seniors a $200 shipboard credit when they charge the cruise to their American Express Senior Card. This is just one of many breaks available only to holders of American Express Senior or Senior Gold cards. For information on how to apply for the card, Tel. 800/297-3429 or apply online at www.americanexpress.com.

World Explorer Cruises offer an AARP discount of 15-20%. You must be an AARP member. At press time, the company is undergoing reorganization but is expected to be providing world cruises again soon. It specializes in offbeat, small ship cruises to unusual and remote locales. Tel. 800/854-3835, www.wecruise.com.

Be a Gentleman Host

If you're a refined gentleman of a certain age, have a neat appearance, and can dance, you can cruise for almost nothing if you're willing to dance with unescorted ladies. As a passenger, you don't have crew status but, as a working passenger, you're also not free to do exactly as you wish. The idea is to share your time evenly among all the single ladies without playing favorites. The best way to connect is with an agency that specializes in cruise ship employment. Fees amount to about $30-$40 per day. In exchange, you get a passenger cabin (not a crew berth), a clothing discount, and perhaps an allowance to cover shipboard incidentals and/or airfare to and from the ship. Preferred ages are between 45 and 72 years old. The leading booking agent for gentlemen hosts is The Working Vacation, Tel. 708/301-7535, www.TheWorkingVacation.com.

SMALL SHIP CRUISES

Shirley Linde, editor of SmallShipCruises.com, gives this advice on getting discounts on cruises. See this website as well for current news and deals.

•Many cruise lines have discounts for persons over age 55 or 65. World Explorer Cruise Line, for example, gives a 20 % discount to members of AARP. Sometimes if a senior citizen is traveling with a younger person, a discount will apply to both fares. If you are a senior, be sure to mention it when you ask about a cruise fare.

•Seniors can save on air fare too. Sometimes the cruise/air package is cheaper; sometimes booking air separately is cheaper. If you don't need air because your departure port is nearby, you can get credit on the airfare if it is built into a package price. Plan as far ahead as possible to get the lowest-priced tickets.

•Cruise lines often have pre or post-cruise Hotel packages that are reasonably priced and can be arranged for at the same time you book your cruise. As you plan your total vacation, tell the cruise line or your agent your entire travel plan including pre- and post-cruise travels. Compare the cruise line's deal with what you can get directly from a hotel. Keep in mind that the cruise package is seamless including transfers from airport to Hotel to the ship. Independent travel involves more hassle and baggage handling, and may cost more too.

•Compare cruise lines. Different ships often go to the same destinations. On the Internet, read about the ships and cruises that go to the destination you are interested in. Compare itineraries, accommodations, programs, shore

---

American Express Benefits

American Express Senior or Senior Gold cards carry a special benefit when you book a trip through American Express. First, you get special rates negotiated by American Express with their many vendors. Second, get a travel credit for $100 to $150 for a trip that costs $2,000 or more. Third, you'll be the first to be notified about upcoming specials. For information on how to apply for the card, apply online at www.americanexpress.com or Tel. 800/528-4800 and keep hitting 0 at each prompt until you get a live operator.

excursions and fares. Some cruise lines have cabins for singles with no single supplement. By comparing, you may find a cruise that offers all you want yet has a wonderfully cheap fare. (Be sure when you compare fares that you know whether shore excursions and port charges are included or not.)

•Always ask about special offers. At SmallShipCruises.com, for example, a monthly column covers latest discounts and special offerings on ships all over the world.

Cruise Line Promotions

Princess, Radisson, Royal Caribbean, Royal Olympic, Seabourn, Silver Seas, Star Clipper, Windjammer and **Windstar** are among those cruise lines that may have a special promotion now and again for seniors. Let your travel agent find the best deal for you.

---

6. Hotels and Lodging

Travelers and stay-at-homes alike can strike gold in this chapter because hotels are not just bedrooms. Senior discounts may apply even in your home town to meals in hotel restaurants, membership in the hotel's fitness club, greens fees at a resort's golf course, or a discount at the hotel's beauty salon. Call local hotels that have these services and ask.

Even if you never travel, you might also need a hotel to house out-of-town guests, to host a family reunion, or you simply want a romantic hotel stay close to home for a break in the same, old routine. You might also stay overnight in a downtown hotel to avoid driving home late after the opera or a show. Just because the hotel is your home city, don't forget that magic phrase, "Senior Discounts."

WHAT A DIFFERENCE A DAY MAKES

Rates as quoted here, in ads and in guidebooks are just a starting point. In the real world, hotel rates vary wildly according to the day of the week, season of the year, and how many unsold rooms are in inventory. Generally, city hotels make most of their money from business travelers who stay Sunday through Thursday, so they offer weekend discounts. Country inns, by contrast, charge a big premium on weekends and holidays but cut rates during the week.

If you are retired and can choose your dates, play this to your advantage. If you can get away only during the week, try a bed and breakfast inn. If you can get away only on a weekend, look into fabulous shopping packages in Chicago or Broadway packages in New York. If you're still in the work force, don't overlook senior discounts for business travel, starting as early as age 50 and becoming easier to find as you reach 55, 60 and 62.

Any day can be a good day for a bargain hunter. Hotel marketers constantly monitor room inventory day by day and sometimes hour by hour, and change pricing accordingly. Since most hotels rely on group bookings, they strive to sell the largest possible block of rooms at the highest possible price. The game is so fast and cutthroat, meeting planners sometimes find themselves looking at one price today and, if they don't grab it, a much higher price tomorrow. On the other hand, leftover rooms may sell at the last minute for a deep discount.

Since meetings are booked weeks, months, and even five years in advance, professional meeting planners must lock in a deal for better or worse. However you, the customer who is looking for only one room, might get a last-minute steal on an unsold room. There is always the danger, of course, that the hotel is so fully booked that you can't get a bed at all, let alone a lowball price. If you absolutely must stay at that hotel on that night, pay the asking price (minus, of course, whatever senior discount you can wangle). However, the traveler who has a choice of dates, a choice of hotels, or both can almost always sleep on Easy Street.

You can (1) get on the phone or Internet as close to the date as possible, and look for last-minute deals; (2) Shop around in person. This can be awkward if you're on foot in a big city, but airports have phone banks where free calls can be made. On interstates it's not difficult to visit two or three motels per exit. Be forewarned, however, that highway motels and airport hotels expect a lot of drop-ins late in the day and they are not likely to cut rates until it's very late. (3) you could stop on the highway at, say, 3 p.m. and start calling motels that are several exits ahead.

To get the best rates, always call hotels directly. Their toll-free central reservations people don't have access to rock-bottom rates. By calling the hotel itself, you may also find that a room is available even though you're told by a reservations center that the hotel is fully booked.

Free booklets filled with discounts are found at every interstate rest stop. Pick up one of each publication and see what's available down the road. Some parlay a discount coupon with a senior discount; others are coupons that can be used by anyone of any age, but may be a better deal that you could get with an age-based discount.

THE AARP/CARP ADVANTAGE
Many hotels offer discounts to AARP members, which means a special break

if you're in your early 50s because most other senior discounts don't apply until you're 55, 60, 62 or even 65. If you travel often and are over 50 but under age 62, it may pay to join AARP solely for these discounts. Tel. 800/424-3410 Monday-Friday 8am-8pm, Eastern Time, www.aarp.org.

Hail to the Natives!

The quickest way for hosts to fill unsold rooms during slow times is to run local or regional newspaper ads or radio spots offering state residents a deal they can't resist. It's commonly used to lure Orlando residents to beach hotels in summer when snowbird bookings are light, or to bring Floridians to the theme parks in the slow seasons spring and fall.

You may not hear about these deals if you live in Pensacola and are headed for Miami, or live in San Diego and want a San Francisco vacation. So, any time you're booking a getaway in your home state, ask if there is a discount for state residents. Don't try to fake it. You may have to prove residence in that state by showing a driver's license, tax or utility bill, or voter registration.

IRREGULAR ANTICS

Have you ever bought socks or underwear that were "factory seconds" or "irregulars" because of a flaw you can't even find? Usually, the socks wear just as well as first quality. Hotels, too, have rooms that are "factory seconds" or not quite up to standard. Often, the flaw is something insignificant, such as the red wine that the last guest spilled on the sofa, or a whirlpool tub that doesn't whirl. It takes chutzpah but if all you want is a clean, decent place to sleep, and you don't mind a room that isn't 100% perfect, ask if the hotel has any rooms that are "off inventory" and available at a discount.

PACKAGE PLOYS

Unfortunately for those who seek rock-bottom prices, the trend in the lodgings industry is toward adding features such as a free breakfast or free greens fees rather than lowering room rates in low seasons. Still, you can take the word "package" to the bank. Some packages are so attractive, you can discard some of the benefits and still come out ahead. A couple from western

New York, for example, bought an Orlando package that included air, rental car and hotels. They flew in, got the car, forfeited the hotel nights because they wanted to stay with relatives, and still had a cheaper trip than if they bought plane tickets and booked a rental car!

Some tips on packages:
•Don't be lured by cheesy gimmicks such as "iced champagne" or a tee shirt. Alcoholic drinks are no bargain if you are teetotal, and tee shirts can be bought almost anywhere for peanuts.

•Read the fine print "Dinner for two" probably means a credit that can be applied to a meal. It's enough to cover the pasta special and a house wine, but if you order cocktails, the steak or lobster, and a bottle of wine, and you'll have a substantial bill.

•Airport transfers could mean anything from personal pickup in a limousine to a voucher that gets you aboard a steamy jitney that doesn't leave the airport until it's full. I once sat in a bus at La Guardia for two hours before it left the airport, and have sweltered in minibuses in the Caribbean that didn't budge until every sardine-size seat was taken. Know what you're getting in that free transfer.

•Always ask about honeymoon packages even if this is your third honeymoon with your fourth spouse. These packages usually mean a few extra perks for no additional price. For example, the Jalousie Hilton in St. Lucie offers a special "Honeyboomer" package for people aged 50 and better. For those in love, it's never an untruth to say you're on your honeymoon.

ALTERNATIVES TO HOTELS
•Modest vacation bungalows that the French called gites rent by the month or season. Contact Provence West Ltd., Tel. 970/226-5444 during business hours, Mountain Time.

•Get a job as a house sitter. You might vacation in a fishing lodge, spend a month in a mansion or a waterfront estate that is closed for the season, or a couple of weeks in a city town house. Depending on the responsibilities that go with the deal, you may also get paid in addition to your housing. Of course, you'll also have obligations beyond those of a carefree tourist. To learn more, send a stamped, self-addressed envelope to Caretaker Gazette,

Box 5887-M, Carefree AZ 85377 or contact www.angelfire.com/wa/care-taker.

•Swap houses with someone from, say, the Tyrolean Alps who wants to visit your part of New Mexico, or stay in a villa in Tuscany while your hosts take over your apartment in Manhattan. Among companies that arrange house swaps are Homelink in Tampa FL, Tel. 800/638-3841; Intervac in California, 800/756-HOME and Trading Homes International, 800/877-8723.

•If you belong to any national organizations, learn if they have a housing program in which members are willing to put up another member for a night or two. The bed and breakfast program by and for members of the American Society of Journalists and Authors, for example, assures free housing for a night or two for writers on book or research tours. Members of the Family Motor Coach Association offer free overnight RV parking for fellow motorhome travelers.

Groups you can join for the sole purpose of offering and receiving hospitality include Women Welcome Women, which is based in England at Tel. 011-44-14-94-46-54-41; The Hospitality Exchange, Tel. 406/538-8770; Evergreen Bed & Breakfast Club (must be aged 50 or better), Tel. 815/456-3111; Affordable Travel Club, Tel. 253/858-2172; and Servas, Tel. 212/267-0152, www.usservas.org. Members live worldwide; U.S. headquarters are in New York.

•Work your way through a great vacation by signing on for a six-month stint at a Club Med. It helps if you speak another language, especially French. You'll clean rooms, babysit, work the shop or the front desk, and participate after hours in rousing stage shows. See www.clubmedjobs.com.

HOTEL AND MOTEL CHAINS
Rates and rules are always subject to change, but here are some discounts to look for. As always, the bywords are ask and keep asking for a senior discount. Either ahead of time or at check-in, be sure to ask what other senior discounts are available in the hotel (restaurants, spa treatments, parking, gift shop, salon).

Note: While the Internet is sometimes the key to the best hotel rates, websites rarely mention senior discounts. If they are not given, use the "contact us" feature to ask specifically about them. Never forget that the diligent seeker of senior discounts often has to dig a little deeper than everyone else.

AmerSuite Inns and Suites offer a discount of 10% to AARP members of any age and to anyone else who is 65 or over. Tel. 800/833-1516, www.amerisuites.com.

Apple Core Hotels are five, moderately-priced, newly renovated hotels in midtown Manhattan. They're a boffo deal at full price and irresistible at 10% off for AARP members. The deal applies to rates of $109 or over; occasional promotions below this rate aren't discounted. Included are La Quinta Inn Manhattan, Red Roof Manhattan, Comfort Inn Midtown, Super 8 Hotel Times Square and the Ramada Inn East Side. You couldn't ask for better locations and some of them throw in a free continental breakfast. Tel. 212/790-2700 or 800/567-7720, www.applecorehotels.com.

Aston Hotels & Resorts number more than 33 properties in the islands of Kauai, Oahi, Maui and the Big Island, Hawaii, so you can stay within the same hotel family if you want to see all the islands. Keep in mind that the value season in this part of the world is April 1 through the end of June and September 1 until just before the Christmas holidays. In any season, however, take 25% off regular rates if at least one person in the room is 50 years old or better. In addition, seniors who stay six nights get the seventh free at participating Astons. Ask too about the ASTONishing Deals program, available to all guests, that provides discount coupons, a buy-one-get-one luau offer, and other perks. From the mainland U.S. and Canada Tel. 800/922-7866; within Hawaii, 800/321-2558, www.aston-hotels.com.

Baymont Inns and Suites provide a 10% discount at age 55. Their website is www.baymontinns.com.

Best Inn and Best Suites is a chain of more than 100 modestly priced motels known for their free breakfast, free local phone calls, and "evergreen" rooms for those who want an environmentally "green" sleep. Seniors aged 50 and over get a 10% discount. AARP membership is not a requirement. Tel 800/237-8466, www.bestinn.com.

Best Western is one of our favorite chains because they don't all look alike. Rooms aren't plush but are very well appointed, usually with coffee maker, one or more premium cable channels, and a few other frills. Usually a continental breakfast goes with the rate, and it has always amounted to a more bountiful meal than we expected, not just the donuts and coffee that constitutes a continental at some places . At most Best Westerns, seniors get a 10% discount and savings are even better if you are also a member of AAA and/or AARP. Get a Gold Crown Club card, a frequent guest program in which credits are given for free room nights. The company also offers rentals of entire homes, some of them with swimming pool. Rent by the week or two and host the kids and grandkids. The senior discount also applies to them. Tel. 800/528-1234, bestwestern.com.

Bolongo Bay Beach Club in the U.S. Virgin Islands has one of the most generous all-inclusive vacations in the islands and it offers additional savings to people aged 50 and over. Ask about the Golden Rewards Program, which knocks at least 15% off a stay of at least five nights. Sail, sun, beachcomb, kayak, work out in the fitness center, take a scuba lesson, and eat like a sultan. Several all-inclusive options are available so find the deal that best suits you. Tel. 800/524-4746.

Budget Host motels are found in more than 160 locations in the United States and Canada, offering two- and three-star accommodations and, in most cases, a continental breakfast. Most offer at-door parking, cable TV with premium channels, in-room coffee, direct dial telephones and a choice of bed sizes. All offer a senior discount but each is different. Rates and discount policies are listed in the free directory, which is available at any Budget Host or Tel. 800/BUD-HOST, www.budgethost.com.

Carlson Hotels Worldwide and Radisson Hotels & Resorts have a Senior Breaks deal that means 25-40% off standard room rates for people aged 50 and over in North America and ages 65 and over in Europe and Australia. The rates apply year-round, seven days a week, based on availability. In addition, many Radisson hotels offer seniors and their parties senior discounts on meals in hotel restaurants, whether or not they are hotel guests. For information: Tel. 800/333-3333, www.radisson.com. **Park Plaza** hotels offer a discount of up to 25% to members of AARP. For information: www.parkplaza.com or Tel. 800/814-7000.

FANTASTIC DISCOUNTS & DEALS FOR ANYONE OVER 50!

Choice Hotels including **Comfort Inns** and **Clarion Inns**, found worldwide, offer a discount of 20-30% for people ages 60 and over and 10% if you're 50 or better. Don't just ask for the "senior" discount. If you're in the upper age category, go for the gold! Tel. 877/424-6423 in the U.S. and Canada, www.ChoiceHotels.com.

Country Inns & Suites by Carlson are found in major cities throughout North America and worldwide. If you're 50 years old or better, these cozy, bed-and-breakfast-style inns knock 10% off regular rates. Breakfast is included for all guests. Tel. 800/456-4000, www.countryinns.com.

Days Inns give a 10% discount off standard published rates if you're 60 or older and can present proof of age. Membership in their senior club, which costs $15 for one year and $50 for five years, gets you a free subscription to their quarterly travel magazine, and discounts on theme parks, airlines, cruises, car rentals, and free local calls at many Days Inn locations. Tel.800/329-7466, www.daysinn.com.

Embassy Suites give a 10% discount to AARP members. If you're not an AARP member, ask what other senior discounts are available. Tel. 800/362-2779, www.embassy-suites.com.

Fairfield Inns give a discount of 10-30% to AARP card holders. Tel. 800/228-2800, www.fairfieldinn.com.

Fairmont Hotels & Resorts worldwide offer a 25% AARP discount off room rates. Members of the Canadian CARP get a discount of 20% off rates for bed and breakfast. For both, a membership card must be shown at check-in. If you're a frequent traveler as well as a seasoned citizen, join Fairmont's loyalty program, the Fairmont President's Club. Membership is free and the more room nights you rack up, the more privileges are laid on. Perks include such things as free access to fitness facilities, room upgrades, no service charge for third-party phone calls and much more. Tel. 800/527-4727, www.fairmont.com

Hampton Inn & Suites call their program Lifestyle 50 Plus. For about $60 a year you get discounts on hotels, rental cars, air fare and cruises booked through the program's toll-free service center. Ask about a trial membership that allows you to try before you buy. If you're a business traveler, the deal could pay for itself quickly. This is one of the best deals that people in their early 50s can get without joining AARP. Tel. 800/204-4033.

Hilton offers its Senior Honors program to persons age 60 and better. Members get half off or more at Hilton hotels worldwide. Since children (usually age 18 and under) sleep free with paying adults, this is a goldmine for people who take their grandchildren on vacation. For information on the program, Tel. 800/432-3600, www.hilton.com. Individual Hiltons also have individual promotions such as the Honeyboomer package offered by the Jalousie Hilton, St. Lucia in the West Indies, for couples ages 50 and over.

Holiday Inns and Holiday Inn Express usually give discounts of 10-40% to persons who are 50 and over. Tel. 800/465-4329, www.holiday-inn.com. One of the best is the Holiday Inn Family Suites and Resort in Orlando, where suites are themed for romance, kids, movie buffs or business. Take the grandkids, and get a private bedroom for yourself, a bedroom for the kids, bath and sitting room for less than many Orlando hotels charge for the room alone. If it's just the two of you on a romantic holiday, the Romance Suite has a heart-shaped Jacuzzi in the living room. Some suites have a full kitchen. An interesting kink here is that discounts kick in at age 60 and get sweeter again at 70 and 80. There are many other sweeteners too, such as free choo-choo rides for the kids, free shuttle rides to the theme parks, and a grand breakfast buffet where kids eat free. For reservations, contact the inn directly, Tel. 407/387-KIDS or 877/387-5437 U.S. and Canads. www.hifamilysuites.com.

Hotel Caravelle on the island of St. Croix is singled out here because senior discounts, especially discounts that apply as early as age 60, are rare in the U.S. Virgin Islands. The hotel is on the waterfront at Christiansted and is a favorite gathering, quaffing and dining spot for locals, mainlanders, and visitors from Denmark. Ask for the best rate, which is about $120 in winter and $95 off season, then ask for the 15% senior discount. Tel. 800/524-0410, www.hotelcaravelle.com.

Howard Johnson motels offer discounts of 10-15% for people 50 and over. Tel. 800/446-4656, www.hojo.com.

Inter-Continental hotels have a "55 for $55" program in participating hotels for at least part of the year. It's a luxury chain, where rooms costing

$200 and more may be available to seniors at this fantastic rate. You'll need photo ID with birth date on check-in, and rates are plus tax and perhaps other fees or charges. AARP members can also get discounts that vary from hotel to hotel. Tel. 800/327-0200 or www.interconti.com.

Kimpton Hotels & Restaurants is a San Francisco-based company known for stylish, boutique hotels with a destination restaurant and celebrity chef. However, none of the 38 hotels is actually named Kimpton, so to learn their names you have to go to the website, www.kimptongroup.com or get a directory (Tel. 800/KIMPTON). The group includes such wonderful hotels as the Hotel Burnham Chicago with its Atwood Café, the chic Hotel Palmar in San Francisco, the Topaz, Rouge, Madera, Monaco and Helix hotels in Washington DC, the Sky Hotel in Aspen, and many more throughout the United States and Canada. Folks 55 and older can get the Young At Heart Rate, ranging from $129 to $239 for spacious, gracious rooms regularly priced at much more. The deal includes a daily wine reception in the lobby and, for seniors, every third night is free. Proof of age must be shown at check-in.

Long Bay Beach Resort & Villas is a 52-acre hillside hideaway overlooking a white sand beach in Tortola, British Virgin Islands. Senior discounts aren't common in the Caribbean, but here vacationers ages 65 and older can check in for close to 50% off regular rates during certain time periods. Stays should be three nights or longer. Breakfast is included in rates. Enjoy live music, the swim-up bar, complimentary tennis clinics and a full spa. Ask about senior rates, monthly or seasonal rates and attractive single occupancy rates. Tel. 877/906-2525, www.longbay.com.

Marriott hotels offer a 15% savings for all seniors ages 62 and better at 2,000 participating Marriott Hotels worldwide. This includes Marriott Hotels and Suites; JW Marriott Hotels and Resorts; Renaissance Hotels, Resorts and Suites; Courtyard; Fairfield Inn; Residence Inn; TownePlace Suites and SpringHill Suites hotels. Discounted rooms are offered on a space-available basis, and a maximum of two rooms can be reserved per stay. There is no limit on the number of nights per stay; Discounts are available seven days a week. Request the discount when making reservations; at check-in guests must present valid identification with date of birth , Tel. 800/228-9290, www.marriott.com. Weekend and other discounts may also be available in preference to, or in addition to, the senior rate.

Outrigger Hotels' Fifty-Plus Program offers travelers age 50 and over discounts of 20-30% off published rates, depending on the hotel and room category. The group, found throughout the Hawaiian islands and known for its luxury hotels and true island hospitality, also has resort condominiums if you're looking for a long-term stay in a fully equipped apartment. The Fifty Plus Program also applies to them. AARP and CARP members can do even better, receiving 25% to 35% savings on select room categories. Proof of age and membership are required at check-in. Tel. 800/462-6262, www.outrigger.com.

Pan Pacific Hotels & Resorts are found in North America, Asia and throughout the Pacific. How about a harbor-view room in Vancouver, a ski vacation on Whistler Mountain, or an exotic vacation in Bangkok, where you are welcomed with a drink and a fruit basket? While Pan Pacific doesn't have a uniform senior discount policy that applies to all hotels all the time, it's definitely worth asking because during special promotions, seniors ages 55 and better can get a $365 room for as little as $160 or a $505 junior suite for $230. Blackout dates apply. Tell your travel agent to ask for senior rates on your behalf. They are commissionable. Proof of age must be shown at check-in. The chain operates 18 hotels in Asia, the Pacific, and North America. Tel. (800) 327-8585, www.panpacific.com.

Park Inn and Park Plaza Hotels are found in more than 100 locations in North America, Europe and the Asia-Pacific region. If you're a member of AARP, ask for a discount, which could be as high as 25% off standard room rates. Tel. 800/670-7275, www.parkhtls.com.

Radisson Hotels & Resorts are found in more than 430 locations in 59 countries. Ask for the Senior Breaks discount, which kicks in at age 50 (at Radissons in the United States and Canada only) and gives discounts of 25-40% off standard rates. Senior Break discounts at the chain's Europe and Australia properties apply after age 65. Most of the hotels also offer a senior discount on meals at off-peak hours, whether or not you're staying at the hotel. Call ahead. Tel. 800/333-3333, www.radisson.com.

Ramada Inns give a discount of at least 15% to AARP members, sometimes as much as 30%. Chain-wide there is no other senior discount for those who are not AARP members but ask anyway. Individual inns may have a deal for you. Tel. 800/772-9467 or 800/2-RAMADA, www.ramada.com.

FANTASTIC DISCOUNTS & DEALS FOR ANYONE OVER 50!

Residence Inns offer a discount of 10-30% to AARP members ages 50 and over. If you're not an AARP member, ask what senior discounts are available. Tel. 800/331-3131, www.residenceinn.com.

Renaissance Hotels will cut room rates up to 50% for AARP members. Discounts also apply to some food and beverage costs, but rules are complicated and you must reserve three weeks ahead. If you're not an AARP member, ask what senior discounts are available. Tel. 800/468-3571, www.renaissancehotels.com.

Select Inns have a program called Select Senior Club in which anyone age 55 and better can join free. Get hotel discounts of 15-25% and get a free night for every eight nights booked. The inns are found in Western states, Tel. 800/641-1000.

Sheraton hotels honor the AARP card by taking 25% off rack rates. If you're not an AARP member but are 55 and over ask about other senior discounts. Tel. 800/325-3535. www.sheraton.com.

Starwood Hotels aren't a household name only because you know them by other names such as Four Points by Sheraton, Westin, Sheraton, W, or the Luxury Collection. Their discount for AARP members is 15-25 percent off rack rates and as much as 50% off if you book three weeks ahead and stay over a Thursday, Friday, and Saturday night. The hotels and resorts are found in 80 countries, so choices are vast. To find a hotel, go to www.starwoodhotels.com, but to get the AARP rate you must Tel. 877/778-2277.

Super 8 Motels give a 10% discount to AARP members, but you have to ask for Code 8800 6955 8025. Tel. 800/800/8000, www.super8.com.

Travelodge Inns, Suites, Hotels, and World Resorts offer a 10% discount to seniors aged 50 and better and 15% to members of AARP. The company also operates **Thriftlodge**, a no-frills chain. In a **Travelodge Inn** you'll get a clean, comfortable room plus in-room coffee, free access to long distance carriers, free incoming faxes, cable TV, and a free newspaper to be picked up in the lobby. A **Travelodge Hotel** offers the same features as the Inns plus a restaurant. The hotel may also have a guest laundry, gift shop, and swimming pool. **Travelodge Suites** have expanded living and working space, sometimes in a separate room. **Travelodge Resorts** offer deluxe accommodations, large pool, on-site restaurant, in-room microwave and refrigerator, free local calls, and other, more upscale features.

If you're a frequent traveler, ask about the Travelodge Miles Guest Rewards Program, for which you can get free stays, airline miles, car rentals, or gift certificates. Tel. 800/878-7878 or, for Thriftlodge, 800/525-9055, www.travelodge.com.

Warner Historic Hotels in England cater exclusively to people ages 55 and older, so they're ideal for seniors who don't want to listen to the patter of little feet. There are six hotels in the chain, all of them mansions or castles that have been converted to four-star hotels. Guests get accommodations, a full English breakfast and a three-course dinner daily. Americans benefit if they are AARP members because they get a 20% discount on wellness activities at all Warner properties. Have a spa treatment, go hot air ballooning, bowl, or play tennis, snooker, croquet or billiards. Cabaret acts entertain nightly at the hotels. Tel. toll-free 866/850-5452, www.warnervacations.com.

Windmill Inns are found only in Arizona and Oregon and you must be 65 or older to join their America's Club. Perks include a $10 room discount and a free night for every nine nights stayed. Tel. 800/547-4747.

Wyndham discounts of 20% start at age 50 if you have an AARP card. Tel. 800/996-3426, www.wyndham.com.

ADDITIONAL WEBSITES
•Stay in a university residence hall in London or elsewhere in the United Kingdom for only about $30 nightly by booking with Rooms are single and have a bed and desk, but do not have a private bath and are available only in summer. Go to www.venuemasters.co.uk.

•If you are traveling solo and the resort or tour charges a singles supplement, go to or to find a travel roommate and you'll each pay half the double rate. Go to travelchums.com or whytravelalone.com.

IS HOUSE SWAPPING FOR YOU?
Stay free this spring in England's lake country. Spend a week in Austria in ski season or a month exploring western Australia. You'll stay at comfortable

digs that feel just like home. In fact, these are homes and the only price you pay to live in them is to let their owners live in your house in exchange. If you're online, you'll have the widest choice, but a few printed directories are available for those who don't use the Internet.

Drawbacks are obvious, so it's important to choose your destination and your tenants with kid-glove care. Still, problems are minimized because you're in each other's houses, in effect holding each other hostage.

The most popular swaps occur between English speaking countries, but that opens a world of possibilities from North America to the British Isles, Australia, and the Caribbean, as well as many nations where English is a second language. Competition can be keen, so start your search months in advance. Finding a match will be easier if you live in a popular area such as Hawaii, New York, San Francisco, Washington DC, close to the ocean, or near some world-famous tourist magnet such as Walt Disney World, the Grand Canyon, Kennedy Space Center, or the Black Hills.

Even if you live in Nowhereville, USA, however, it's possible to find people who will give you a villa in the south of France in return for a stay in the suburbs, or on a farm, or in a city apartment in Minneapolis. You never know until you try.

Expect to pay fees of about $30 to $120 per year to be listed in a house-swap website, directory or both. In some cases, lifelong friendships and repeat visits result. Or, pay dues again next year and find a new swap in another part of the world. Try:

- HomeLink, or 800/638-3841, www.swapnow.com
- Intervac, or 800/756-4663, www.intervac.com
- HomeExchange.com or 805/898-9660
- International Home Exchange Network, or 407/862-7211, www.ihac.com
- Vacation Homes Unlimited, or 800/848-7927, www.exchangehomes.com
- Trading Homes International, or 800/877-8723, www.trading-homes.com

Seniors who go to www.wiredseniors.com can also click on a home exchange network that costs $65 for a three-year membership or, if you belong to AARP or CARP, $45 for three years. Life membership is $100. Homes are available worldwide.

And Ye Shall Find Rest

If you're a retired pastor or missionary, members of the Christian Hospitality Network offer discounts at more than 600 inns worldwide. Open to the traveling public of all faiths, these are not religious businesses per se. They operate like any other commercial enterprises except that owners or hosts want to give a special price break to people in God's service. Accommodations range from simple motels on major highways to cottages to castles. First, go to the website or request a brochure, and decide where you want to stay. When booking, identify yourself as a church worker and ask what discount is available. Tel. 865/376-7546, www.ChristianHospitalityNetwork.com.

TAKE THE GRANDKIDS TO FRANCE

Country Cottages sells packages that include airfare, a rental car, hotels and a stay in a private home in Provence. A recent 11-night package package provided two nights in a hotel in Paris, a week in a country villa, a car for a week, and round-trip air from the United States for only $999 per person in a group of eight. Best of all, grandparents and grandchildren in parties of six or more get a $50 per person discount!

Based in Florida, this travel packager can find you a cottage, townhouse, manor house or even the castle of your dreams in France. All have modern kitchen and bath furnished with linens, towels and everything needed for cooking plus a caretaker on call to solve any problems. The company can create almost any package that suits your needs, including add-on nights in Paris or longer stays in the villas or cottages. Tel. 800/674-8883, www.villacentral.com.

7. Services and Associations

Even though most of these listings are familiar national and international names, many do not have a toll-free consumer number. To find whether one is in your city, check the White or Yellow Pages or go to the website.

American Association of Grandparents is a membership organization for those who pay dues. Look into its benefits and, if you join, keep track of your spending on their website. Pop-up ads offer oceans of goods and services. After you've spent $1,000, your dues are refunded. American Association of Grandparents, 3220 N Street N.M. #281, www.internetgrandparents.com.

American Express cards offer long lists of extras that aren't found in everyday credit cards. For the American Express Senior Card, the cost is $35 (the regular card costs $55), and the fee is also reduced for each additional card issued to the account. The American Express Senior Gold Card is only $55 a year to seniors plus $25 for each additional card. Non-seniors pay $75 yearly for the Gold Card. With senior membership, you get a magazine three times a year, a generous credit if you book a trip costing $2,000 or more, 24-hour customer service, special access to events tickets, free travel checks, special savings galore, and all the conveniences, prestige and protection that an American Express card provides at home and abroad. Tel. 800/297-3429, www.americanexpress.com.

American WholeHealth fitness centers have more than 25,000 member practitioners who give a discount of five-30 % on acupuncture, massage, yoga, personal training, chiropractic services and the use of fitness equipment. AARP members check it out at www.aarp.org/alternatives. If you're not an AARP member but are 55 or older, ask what discounts are available. Tel. 888/893-4739.

Auto Insurance from **The Hartford** is discounted for AARP members. Tel. 800/972-9922, www.aarpautoinsurance.com.

Burgess Boys Car and Truck Centers in Wisconsin offer a senior discount and a free ride home if you must leave your vehicle there for service. Check the local phone directory for Burgess Boys locations.

Carpet Cleaning is almost all in the hands of small, individually owned, local businesspeople. We were unable to find any national chains that offer a uniform senior discount. Competition in many areas has become so fierce, seniors have to step lively to avoid being scammed by low-ball bids or swamped by carpet cleaning telemarketers. Still, senior discounts are abundant and easy to find through local ads. Our advice is to get an in-home quote in writing, specifying every service for every carpet including (1) the hallway that is only two feet long but still incurs a charge for a hall, (2) the area in front of the couch because they'll say it has extra soil and needs additional stain treatment, and (3) the protective coating they will certainly try to sell you after you have agreed on a price for the cleaning. Get a complete quote, then ask if a senior discount applies on top of that.

Dry Cleaning remains primarily a locally-owned industry and we weren't able to find any chains that offer an across-the-board senior discount. However, discounting abounds at the local level. Call around and check before deciding where to take your clothes. Discounts are usually only for certain garments or for certain days.

Escrow Officer Fees are paid for seniors who buy into one of sixteen communities in western Nevada in an area said to be "above the fog and below the snow/" Sites of up to five acres sold by Grass Valley Homes and Land are available. Visit www.oro.net/~golfhome.com.

Fantastic Sam's hair styling salons throughout North America offer a 10 % discount to seniors aged 60 and over Monday-Friday 8 :30am to 3pm. Call ahead to verify each location's discount policy, hours, and to clarify what services qualify for the discount. It may apply only to a haircut.

Gold's Gym is the largest chain of gyms in the world, with outlets throughout North America and other continents. If you follow a workout regiment wherever you go, here's a way to get consistent service as you travel. Gyms are individual owned, so policies differ in regard to ages, but the senior discount is 25 % off monthly fees and 50 % off entry fees. Tel. 800/457-5375, www.goldsgym.com.

Great Clips is a chain of almost 1,800 hair salons throughout the United States and Canada. Walk-ins are welcome here and people ages 65 and older get $1-$3 clipped off the price of a haircut. The deal varies with each franchisee, so try calling ahead. Look in local Yellow Pages or find your nearest Great Clips at www.greatclips.com.

Insurance for burial, whole life, and term life is a specialty at Senior American Insurance, which claims it can come up with the best quotes for older Americans. If you want to give them a try, Tel. 716/894-4020, 800/332-7557, www.senioramericanins.com.

Internet service is available through Safenet2000.com for $17.95 per month, paid semi-annually, for those who are aged 50 and better. There is no limit on the hours spent online and the service costs the same whether you choose a filtered or non-filtered service (although not all numbers can get the sophisticated filter feature). Many of the company's customers are home schoolers and libraries, so filtering out unsuitable emails is a priority with them. The senior discount is available only by phone, Tel. 508/643-0581.

AARP members get a 10 % discount on a variety of Internet Service Providers including Prodigy, CompuServe and AOL. Sovernet.com offers Internet service for 20 % off to people 65 and over. Go through the AARP member services center, using your membership number.

Jenny Craig diet centers are found at more than 600 locations in the United States, Canada, Australia, New Zealand and Puerto Rico. The company's unique weight loss plan includes 70 specialty food products, all of them formulated to make dieting a snap. At corporate-owned locations, people aged 65 and over can get a 10 % discount on foods on Wednesday and Thursday. Check the White or Yellow Pages, then call your local Jenny Craig. Tel. 800/597-JENNY or 800/JENNY-CARE, www.jennycraig.com.

Jiffy Lube auto service centers are found at more than 2,200 locations in the United States and Canada. Check the Yellow Pages for your local center, then call ahead to ask about the senior discount. It's usually 10 % but ages vary. Centers can also be found or contacted through www.jiffylube.com.

Liberty Benefits offer health, pharmacy and medical benefits to people ages 50-65. A variety of plans are available, all paid monthly at $14.95 to $44.95

per month. The higher the premium, the more extensive the coverage. If you're too young for Medicare, here's a way to get limited coverage without a physical exam or exclusions for pre-existing conditions. Tel. 800/479-5653, www.libertybenefits.com.

Meineke Muffler shops in some cities offer a 20 % discount to people ages 60 and over, often through participation in local Golden Age discount programs. Call ahead.

Midas Auto Service Experts auto service centers, found nationwide, offer seniors a 10 % discount off parts and service. Policies vary, so phone ahead. Find your local center in the Yellow Pages or go to www.midas.com.

Myofascial Pain Release centers are found in Sedona AZ , Tel. 928/282-3002, where the clinic is called Therapy on the Rocks, and in Paoli PA, where it's called the Myofascial Release Treatment Center Tel. 610/644-0136. For either, Tel. 800/327-2425. Both centers offer the same, hands-on treatments for stress-related pain or movement dysfunction that have not responded to traditional medical care. Men and women ages 65 and over get hands-on treatments at half price, which is $120 per hour (versus $120 per half-hour) including use of the whirlpool.

Nutri-Lawn is a yard care chain that offers a 5% discount to seniors. Check your phone book to see if there's one in your city, then call to ask about the senior discount.

Orlando visits cost far less when you know that the I-Ride Trolley Service serves a 14-mile route that includes the entire International Drive area (hotels, shopping, dining, attractions and the Convention Center), Sea World, Universal Boulevard, Wet 'n Wild, and a couple of must-see outlet malls. Leave your car at your hotel to avoid hassle, traffic, crowding, and high parking fees at theme parks and conventions. If you arrive by plane, take a cab or one of the shuttles to your hotel in the I-Drive area and use the trolley for everyday travel. A rental car isn't necessary. Air-conditioned trolleys run every day 8am to 10:30pm and seniors aged 65 and better pay only 25 cents per ride. Www.IRideTrolley.com.

Overhead Door Company showrooms and service centers offer a 5 % senior discount on garage doors and service. See your local Yellow Pages or go to www.ohdkc.com to see if there is one in your city.

Personal Liability Umbrella Policies are greatly discounted by State Farm Insurance for some couples in which one spouse is 50 years old. Some restrictions apply and the discount isn't available to households that have youthful drivers. Such policies, usually written for $1 million or more, cover additional liability for homeowner and auto policies.

St. Louis/St. Charles MO area seniors are fortunate to have the Gateway Seniors Association, a non-profit group that screens businesses that offer a senior discount, and maintains an up-to-date list. Local seniors can get the list free, then search for the desired service. Businesses pay to participate. The long list includes accountants, attorneys, auto repair shops, heating/air conditioning companies, oral surgeons, kennels, moving and storage companies, picture framing, satellite television, photographers, ad inf. It's then up to you, the senior, to find a participating provider and sort out all the rules and details. Tel. 639/922-2551, www.gsainfo.org.

Saturn is the only auto dealership we've found that offers a senior discount. It's 10 % off parts and service for ages 55 and older, and it may not be available at every dealership. Call to ask.

ServiceMaster is a national chain of home care specialists who are licensed and guarantee their work. Names include TruGreen and ChemLawn yard care services, Terminix for termites, Brink's Home Security burglar alarms, Merry Maids, Rescue Rooter, Furniture Medics and others. If there's ServiceMaster member in your phone book, it's likely you can call any hour of the day or night to get help with home repairs, yard service, or emergency services such as carpet rescue, fire recovery or a stopped-up drain. Always ask if a senior discount is available, and sign on at the website for news of individual specials that vary by service and by region. Tel. 888-WE-SERVE, www.ServiceMaster.com.

SuperCuts is a hair salon chain with almost 1,000 locations throughout North America. Deals vary, but people aged 60 and up can usually get $2 off the price of haircut. Check the White Pages or find a location at www.supercuts.com.

Discounts on Everything!

With one phone call, you can learn about a wide range of senior discounts in your city, ranging from 5 % on plumbing repairs to 10% off at the hardware store on Tuesdays, to 15% or more on goods and services ranging from haircuts to a new kitchen floor!

It all begins with your local Council on Aging, Chamber of Commerce, or Senior Citizens Center. Someone, usually a volunteer, calls on merchants and service people asking them to give a discount to seniors. Each business creates its own policy regarding the amount of the discount, at what age it applies, and other rules regarding when and how the discount can be claimed. In return, the business gets free mention in the sponsoring organization's websites, newsletters, bulletin boards and so on. You, the smart shopper who is 50 or older, will naturally patronize places that give discounts, so *voila!*, it's a win-win situation for both you and the business community.

Call the local Chamber of Commerce or Council on Aging today to see if your city has such a program. You may need to join a group, sign up for a card (usually free or very low cost) or find a list of participating businesses in a newspaper or on the Web.

Travel Packages from two superb vacation providers, Globus and Cosmos, are discounted $50 for AARP members. Offering itineraries in 70 countries, these packagers provide a seamless vacation with reservations, airfare, accommodations, meals, local transportation and guides, luggage transfers and other time savers. Globus vacations are the more structured, while Cosmos tours combine the convenience of group travel with much more free time and meals on your own. Tel. 866/285-9182.

Travel Writing is a wonderful pursuit as you get older and have more time (and perhaps less money) to travel. Gordon Burgett's Travel Writer's Guide, How to Earn Thrice What You Spend on Travel by Writing Magazine and Newspaper Articles is available in print and digital form from Tel. 800/563-1454, www.sops.com or e-mail gordn@sops.com. Priced at $17.95 plus shipping for print or $15.95 in Word format, Burgett's book is offered at a 10% discount to seniors who mention this book.

FANTASTIC DISCOUNTS & DEALS FOR ANYONE OVER 50!

Zip Lube is a New Mexico chain of auto service centers, where a 10 % discount is given to seniors ages 55 and over. Check ahead because individual centers may have a different policy. See local White Pages or go to www.ziplube.com.

Red Alert!

Just because you click on a link to a product or service advertised on a senior citizen website, it doesn't mean you're getting a special discount. It just means the advertiser paid to buy senior viewers. A website that reports legitimate senior discounts is www.seniordiscounts.com, which you must search by city. Listings are free, whether or not the product or service is an advertiser, and there is tremendous variety in your city. Also try www.wiredseniors.com, which lists individual motels, B&Bs, condos and villas worldwide. It takes time to find the right stay in the right locale, but it's fun to see what is available, where. The website's online shopping mall also lists many products for which a senior discount is automatic when you click on the link to them from the senior website. Most of the deals are available online only.

---

8. Never Too Old to Learn

Continuing education for fun, profit and even advanced degrees is a passion with many seniors. Once introduced to an Elderhostel or InterHostel vacation, many people never go back to ordinary travel. Your own hometown is the place to begin your search for a fantastic deal on learning. Visit local colleges' admissions offices and you'll find a wide choice of classes ranging from full-credit courses (often offered to seniors at a discount) to short courses, TV courses, night school, educational trips and cruises, and courses designed strictly for seniors.

Don't worry if you don't have a high school diploma or G.E.D. Even at the college level, many courses are available to those who simply want to learn, not necessarily pursue a degree.

Libraries often offer free or low-cost courses; library bulletin boards are a good place to look for announcements of upcoming courses, workshops and seminars. Since almost every college and university has something of interest to seniors, it's impossible to list them all. However, here are some sample deals plus deals for seniors who travel.

Algonquin College in Ottawa, Ontario allows people ages 60 and over to register for funded Continuing Education courses that cost only $20. Request the brochure to see which courses are available. Tel. 613/727-9797.

Cornell Laboratory of Ornithology in cooperation with Wild Birds Unlimited asks the help of backyard bird watchers in taking regular census. The annual Great Backyard Bird Count held each February contributes immeasurably to knowledge of various species' numbers and movements. There is no fee to register; novices and experts are recruited. You don't have to know a titmouse from a bald eagle. You'll be instructed in how to help and will make a lot of friends along the way. Tel. 800/843-2473, www.birdsource.org.

FANTASTIC DISCOUNTS & DEALS FOR ANYONE OVER 50!

The Corporation for National and Community Service is the organization that runs programs such as RSVP (Retired and Senior Volunteer Program), the Foster Grandparent Program for seniors who work with children, and the Senior Companion Program in which seniors aid adults who need extra assistance. Learn more than you ever thought possible about yourself by sharing your time with those in need. Tel. 800/424-8867, www.seniorcorps.com.

Elderhostel is an international program with an exciting list of opportunities to travel and learn. You might travel by boat, or fly or drive to a campus where you'll stay in a dorm and take a course, or even travel in your own RV in a convoy with other Elderhostel participants, studying history and nature along the way. It's nothing like the grind you went through in school. These courses range from the jazz age to watercolor, poetry to sailing. Pick a subject that relates to your current lifestyle, interests, or retirement dreams. You'll meet wonderful folks who share your interests. Costs vary greatly depending on transportation, meals, and accommodations as well as course supplies. When Elderhostels are held in your home town, you can attend as a day student if you prefer. www.elderhostel.org.

InterHostel is a program of the University of New Hampshire designed for people anywhere (not just New Hampshire residents) who are over 50 want to travel and learn. Groups go on trips in the United States and abroad with experts in such fields as food and wine, history, literature or the sciences. Groups are small; schedules are designed for seniors who are healthy and fairly active. Costs vary greatly, but a 13-night adventure in France costs $3,200 per person including air fare from a gateway city, meals with wine, excursions, instructors and lodgings in three- and four-star hotels. If you're alone, the single supplement is only $400. If you want to be matched with a roommate, InterHostel will make every effort to find you one. Only one or two trips to each locale are scheduled each year, so reserve early. Tel. 800/733-9753 in the U.S.; elsewhere 603/862-1146, www.learn.unh.edu/interhostel.

Minnesota residents who are 62 and older can audit courses at the University of Minnesota free or take courses for credit at $9 per credit as long as space is available on the first day of class. Under the plan, seniors don't have to pay student services fees but must pay any required lab or materials fees. Registration for the Senior Citizen Education Program is held on the second day of classes, but you can attend the first day to see if space is available and to learn the routine. Late registration fees are waived for the first two weeks. Tel. 612/624-1111, http://onestop.umn.edu/refistrar.

Princess Cruises' ScholarShip At Sea program combines luxury cruising with opportunities to learn new skills. Take a course in cooking, computers and web page design, finance, digital travel photography, watercolor techniques or even pottery. The Coral Princess even has a pottery studio and kilns on board! Fees for courses start at only $10. Princess doesn't offer age-based discounts, but has loads of price breaks for couples, groups and singles. Since high season usually coincides with school holidays, seniors who are free to travel any time can take advantage of off-season fares, early booking discounts and last-minute specials. Tel. 800/PRINCESS, www.princess.com.

Royal Olympic Cruises have Cultural Enrichment Programs that turn an ordinary cruise into a learning experience. In addition to exciting, world-wide itineraries, the line brings experts on board to give programs in gourmet food preparation and appreciation, archaeology, international affairs, astronomy, environment, and music appreciation. Cruises last three to 55 days and sail out of American and overseas ports. See your travel agent or Tel. 800/872-6400, www.royalolympiccruises.com.

Sail your way through a Semester at Sea with the Institute for Shipboard Education. Primarily a college-level course and cruising adventure, the Institute accepts up to 40 senior adults each session to sail with a faculty of 65 and 600 college students. While cruising you'll call at rural villages, archaeological sites, museums, universities and concert halls.

The down side is that a semester is a long time, requiring a commitment of two-three months of your time plus a good chunk of your money. Rates start at about $11,000 for a summer cruise to about $18,000 for the fall itinerary. Considering that this includes a cabin, all meals, tuition for college credit and the cruise of a lifetime, the price looks far better. Go to www.semesteratsea.com.

SeniorNET.org offers selected discounts including a two-for-one offer on **eBay classes.** If you're downsizing now that the nest is empty, learning your way around eBay is one way to maximize the price you get for your cast-offs.

Sell anything from antimacassars to zithers without leaving the house or having strangers paw your goods at a yard sale.

Senior Summer School programs are available in half a dozen universities in the United States and Canada. Live in a dorm while taking courses that last two-six weeks. Classes and field trips are an extension of each participating university and are taught by highly qualified instructors. Classes are open to everyone, from those who never attended college to those with advanced degrees. Side trips to local attractions are also offered at a modest additional cost. Tel. 800/84-SCHOOL or 800/847-2466, www.seniorsummerschool.com.

State Colleges and Universities as well as many private colleges often have a senior program that allows older citizens to audit course free or to take courses for credit at a highly discounted rate. SUNY, the State University of New York, for example, allows senior citizens to audit courses, park, and participate at highly discounted fees. Call the registration office at any college or university in the United States or Canada and ask about auditing, senior programs, and continuing education classes.

9. Attractions & Theme Parks

Few museums, attractions, amusement parks and theme parks do NOT offer a senior discount. A notable exception is Walt Disney World in Orlando. While they offer many deals throughout the year there is no everyday, senior discount like that offered everywhere else.

If there is a theme park in your future, check ahead not just about a senior discount but the cost of an annual pass. It's usually a blockbuster deal, costing about the same as two, one-day admissions, and many parks offer it at a senior discount to boot. Visit as often as you like to enjoy the music and acts, stroll the gardens, shop the shops. An added plus of an annual pass is that you get in free every time you take visiting family members to the park. Sea World of Orlando, for example, charges $79.95 per year for a pass but seniors ages 55 plus and get one for $64.95! That's less than admission for two days and you don't have to buy a ticket every time you take guests to the park!

Ask About 'Satellite' Parks!

Many theme parks, including Silver Springs and Six Flags, have adjoining or satellite parks, often water parks, that require separate admission. Senior rates and passes are available at them too.

Hundreds of theme parks, attractions and amusement parks are found throughout the United States and Canada and only a smattering are listed here. It's a sure bet a senior discount is available. To check ahead, do an Internet search for the name of the theme park, then keep clicking until you find the schedule of admissions prices, which will include prices and age limits for seniors. Here is just a sample of attractions that give you a lulu of a day and a senior discount too.

Cedar Point on Lake Erie in Ohio is more than a theme park. It's a lakeside paradise with beige satin beaches and a big marina, an historic hotel where Caruso once sang, a campground, and theme park filled with rides and shows. It's the home of The Dragster, the highest, fastest coaster in the world, plus a galaxy of coasters from nostalgic woodies to high-tech rides that dare you to try them. Seniors ages 60 and up pay $29.95 for a one-day ticket compared to $43.95 for other adults. Tel. 419/627-2350, www.cedarpoint.com.

Cypress Gardens has been a mid-Florida fixture since the depression days of the 1930s and it was a shock to the entire state when it closed abruptly in 2003. At press time there is talk of reopening the park. If a new buyer operates it as it was, discounts start at age 55. Seniors can get an annual pass for under $70, which is a superb deal for people who live nearby because the gardens change dramatically with the seasons. Many locals visit at least once a week because this is one of the world's greatest botanical gardens. Tel. 877/595-0509, www.CypressGardens.com.

Disneyland in California will knock $2 off the admission price for people aged 60 and over, www.disneyland.com.

Dollywood's regular admission is $39 but for seniors ages 60 and up it's $35.70. A project of popular country singer Dolly Parton, the park has entertainment galore as well as food, rides and shopping. It's in Pigeon Forge TN, www.dollywood.com. An adjoining water park, Splash and Play, is open seasonally. Adults pay $62.45 while senior admission is $54.65. Additional days are $15 for anyone and combination tickets to both parks are available.

Kennedy Space Center Visitor Complex is one of the United States most visited attractions, an awesome trip into space reality of yesterday, today and tomorrow. From an observation platform you can watch pieces being assembled for the next lift-off to the space station, and throughout the complex you'll see history-making spacecraft, equipment, and astronaut suits that were once the focus of evening news shows.

KSC used to be a free attraction where visitors paid piecemeal for bus tours and IMAX movies. Now admission is charged, but the value is actually better because of the many things that are included in the price. Arrive early and stay the entire day to get your money's worth. There are only two admission prices, adult and child, but families of six or more get a discount. Tel. 321/ 449-4444, www.kennedyspacecenter.com.

Knott's Berry Farm in California knocks $10 off the price of admission if you're aged 60 and over, www.knottsberryfarm.com.

Legoland in Carlsbad CA has more than 50 rides plus shows and hours of fun for the entire family. Regular adult admission is $41.95; seniors ages 60 and above pay $34.95, which is also the price paid by kids ages 2-12, $34.95. Tel. 877/LEGOLAND, www.legoland.com.

Sea World parks are found in Orlando, San Diego and other locations. Seniors aged 55 and over can get a 12-month pass for about $15 less than other adults pay for an annual pass. Such passes are a bonanza, costing less than two, one-day admissions to the parks. Prices vary according to the park. Go to www.seaworld.com.

Silver Springs near Ocala, Florida is another old-Florida attraction that had to make huge improvements to compete with the razzle-dazzle of nearby Orlando, but it hasn't forgotten its reason for being: crystal springs flowing into a river, towering live oaks draped with Spanish moss, native flowers and creatures, and folksy shopping, dining, and shows that bring in some of the biggest name in country music. Seniors ages 55 and better can buy a pass for an entire year for less than the cost of one day at Walt Disney World! Best of all, passes are good for concerts as well as on ordinary days. And parking is free to season pass holders! You won't find a more peaceful setting to amble day after day. Bask by the springs, sit under a tree to read, see seasonal blooms, and visit the animals for an ever-changing show. Tel. 352/236-2121, www.silversprings.com.

Six Flags Parks are found in a dozen states. Senior discounts are impressive but vary a great deal, from age 55 to 62, and according to regular adult admission. At some parks, people aged 70 and up get in free. Call ahead or visit the website, www.sixflags.com.

FANTASTIC DISCOUNTS & DEALS FOR ANYONE OVER 50!

Universal Studios in Florida and California offer a discount on senior admission and passes. Go to www.universalstudios.com.

GETTING YOUR $ WORTH AT THEME PARKS

If you haven't visited a modern theme park lately, prepare yourself for sticker shock. Even with a senior discount, a couple can easily spend $200 a day on admissions, one meal, snacks and a modest souvenir. Parking is usually extra and there is no senior discount on that (although some parks offer free or discounted parking to annual or multi-day pass holders). The good news is that today's theme parks offer quality and quantity beyond compare. Spend as long as you like riding rides, seeing shows, and enjoying fabulous gardens, strolling musicians, parades, street performers, and the passing crowds.

Here are some tips on getting the most from theme parks without busting the budget:

•At most theme parks, visitors are not permitted to take in coolers, food or drink. You can probably get away with a water bottle and some pocket snacks, but it's likely you'll have to buy everything you eat and drink. However, it can pay to call ahead. Some parks, such as the U.S. Space Center in Huntsville, not only permit picnicking, they provide picnic tables in a shaded grove.

•Agree ahead of time on spending limits, especially if you're attending with grandchildren who will start wheedling for souvenirs and treats the moment you arrive.

•Have a good breakfast before leaving home or your hotel. Food at theme parks is premium priced.

•Consider renting a stroller even for older grandchildren, as long as they'll fit, or a wheelchair for anyone who is even slightly mobility impaired. There is a lot of walking and a lot of standing in line.

•Take plenty of film or disposable cameras, sun screen, a sun hat, and rain gear if there is any chance of a shower. Items purchased inside a theme park are usually hugely overpriced.

•Call ahead to make sure you understand in-out privileges. At Walt Disney World, for example, a one-day ticket is good for one park, one day, but multi-day passes allow you to visit multiple parks in one day. You can spend, say, morning at Epcot, go to one of the water parks for the hottest part of the day, then return to Epcot for dinner and the evening fireworks. Walt Disney World Resort offers easy passage from one park to another via free, Worldwide transportation; at others it's a long walk to and from the parking lot, so it isn't practical to bounce in and out.

•Where possible, arrive at the park with tickets because entry lines can be very long. Often tickets can be arranged through your hotel, through your travel agent when you purchase a package, or purchased at an official welcome center. Real tickets (not vouchers) are available online from www.amusementpark.com. Never buy tickets from street vendors. They could be stolen or counterfeit.

•If your hotel offers a free shuttle to the park, consider taking it. You'll save the time and cost of parking and will be dropped off closer to the entrance. There is a definite plus in staying at Disney hotels while visiting the theme parks of Walt Disney World Resort, and at one of the Universal hotels while visiting Universal theme parks. Both offer free, frequent rides among hotels and parks.

•If you're hosting your grandchildren, watch those video games, batting cages, and games of chance at theme parks where you are paying a high price per day for free shows and rides. Coin-op games can be played elsewhere for no admission charge.

•Not every attraction is like those theme parks where one tickets buys all rides and shows for the day. Do a little homework ahead of time. Often, admission to an amusement park is free or very cheap, but every ride costs extra. Seniors who want a short visit or are selective about rides might find piecemeal pricing a better deal.

•Take time to smell the roses. One day isn't enough at such blockbuster attractions as the Henry Ford Museum and Greenfield Village near Detroit, Colonial Williamsburg, or Universal Studios Orlando, but many visitors swear off after one exhausting day because they tried to do it all. Many shows and rides are worth doing more than once, not to mention the many changes that take place in most parks each week, month or season: new shows, new performers or interpretive characters, new menus, one-time special shows, and an ever-changing panorama in beautifully landscaped grounds.

10. Off Your Rocker: Sports and Games

Today's seniors are in their prime in their 50s and 60s and many stay active and even triple-threat competitive well into their 70s, 80s and 90s. Chances are you already know of local games, leagues, and classes where folks over 50 gather for baseball or soccer games, shuffleboard, basketball, water aerobics, tap dancing, kick boxing, yoga or tai chi. Your city is filled with them.

If you compete in a sport, it's likely your state has an annual Olympics or Golden Age Games. In Arizona, for example, the Flagstaff Senior Olympics are held for men and women each September. California has its Running Springs Winter Games and Florida's annual Golden Age Games have been a tradition in Sanford since the 1970s.

Check with your local YM/YWCA, senior center, or Council on Aging to find out how to connect with these competitions in your state. Through them, you may also learn about state and national meets from associations connected with your sport such as track, sky diving, weight lifting, skiing and so on. If you aren't aware of such an association, do an Internet search under Association+ the name of the activity, or ask a reference librarian to do one for you. No matter how rare your sport or hobby, it's likely there's an association for you.

On the national level, the National Senior Games Association holds meets every other year. On an international scale, the Huntsman World Senior Games attract athletes from all over the world to competitions held in Utah.

The Internet and your travel agent can find dozens of tours, adventures and treks that are organized especially for active people over age 50, but we don't list them here because they don't fit the specific "discount" promise of this book.

Here is a sampling of opportunities for those who still have the right stuff and want to exercise it at modest prices:

American WholeHealth fitness centers have more than 25,000 member practitioners who give a discount of five-30% on acupuncture, massage, yoga, personal training, chiropractic services and the use of fitness equipment. AARP members check it out at www.aarp.org/alternatives. If you're not an AARP member but are 55 or older, ask what discounts are available. Tel. 888/893-4739.

Elderhostel has many types of active programs including bicycle, walking, and hiking tours in North America and abroad. On bike tours. Bicycles and repair kits are provided, and groups are accompanied by a "sag" van that carries luggage and any bikers who have reached the end of their pedal power. On walking tours, daily treks are kept modest, but you'll need to be fit enough to cover six to ten miles daily. Accent is on local scenery and culture. Stays are in small hotels; meals are included. Tel. 877/426-8056, www.elderhostel.org.

ElderTreks is an adventure travel company for travelers 50 who want to go to the ends of the earth. From the Gobi Desert in Mongolia to the Peruvian Andes in South America, from the glacial wilds of the Antarctic to the midnight sun of the high Arctic, they'll get you there with a small group of other seniors. Trips to all seven continents are available, with a limit of 16 people per group. Programs are all-inclusive; focus is on local nature and culture. Tel. 416/588-5000, or 800/741 7956, ext. 114, www.eldertreks.com.

Explorations in Travel is for women ages 40 and up. Hiking and canoe adventures are offered in North America and abroad. Some tours are for women over 40 and their daughters or grand-daughters under age 21. Tel. 802/257-0152 during Eastern business hours, www.exploretravel.com.

Fitness Clubs may offer a senior discount, so check the Yellow Pages and call centers closest to your home. Membership is usually a must for those who work out regularly or who follow a consistent discipline in cardiac or lower back rehab, yoga or swimming, or who are loyal to one brand of machines.

However, fitness centers are notorious for scams that start with a long contract and/or a big fee in advance. Once you're hooked, the center may leave town or go bankrupt. Few will give a refund under any circumstances. Check with the Chamber of Commerce and Better Business Bureau to see if the club has had any unresolved complaints filed against it. Read the contract carefully, especially in regard to your rights if you choose to quit the program early.

Whether you are a stay-at-home or are a traveler who requires membership in a nationwide chain, the best deal is YMCAs, which offer a hefty price break for seniors ages 50 and better. Policies vary regionally, but in one central Florida Y, senior singles can join for $23 a month compared to $30 for non-seniors; senior couples pay $35 monthly compared to $42 for a non-senior couple or family. Members can use the swimming pools, fitness center and other facilities. Most Ys around the world offer reciprocal privileges, so you can join at home and use any Y facilities anywhere free or for a token fee.

Bally Fitness is a popular, well established, international chain that is ideal for travelers. While most outlets don't offer a senior discount (call your local Bally's and ask), they have a special break for people who sign up online. Go to www.ballyfitness.com/join and sign up for a pay-as-a-you-go program. Unlike 36-month contracts required at Bally's centers, the online deal lets customers cancel at any time with no penalty.

It isn't well known, but many hotels and resorts offer club memberships to local residents. Pay by the year for access to the workout equipment, spa, swimming pool, beach, tennis courts, and/or other facilities. It costs nothing to call and ask. With a little added chutzpah, you might even wangle a senior discount, especially if you're willing to accept limited access (e.g. agree to go only on weekends, only on weekdays, or to avoid periods when the resort is fully booked.). Hotels are hurting in the present economy and may be interested in locals like yourself as an added source of revenue. Ask the operator to put you through to the manager of recreation facilities, tennis manager, or general manager.

Grand Circle Tours is best known for its luxury tours for people over 50, but the company also offers bicycle tours at home and overseas. Tours are rugged but are toned down for the adventurous traveler over 50. Tel. 800/248-3737, www.gct.com.

Sailors who are 55 and over can get a 10% discount off the FaMet ReeFurl Sail Handling System. The company makes systems for both jib and mains'l.. Owners Tamera and Ron Peterson will also throw in free shipping on orders from seniors. The system is a great help in sail handling as one gets older. Tel. 785/842-0585, www.fametreefurl.com.

Skiing discounts are found everywhere for seniors, but we can't list every ski deal in North America so you'll have to do some homework depending on where you want to ski, when. The schedule of discounts is extremely complex and it's different at every resort. Get a price break on lift tickets on some days of the week or in early and late seasons, and perhaps an additional break on ski trails, rentals or instruction and/or other resort features such as ice skating. Discounts usually start at age 60 or 62, rarely younger, and may get better at age 70 or higher. In fact, some resorts give people over 70 a totally free ride any time!

For example, Wintergreen Resort in the Blue Ridge Mountains of Virginia offers discounts for ages 65 and up on ski lift tickets and ski rentals during weekdays at the height of the season. At the breathtaking Whistler ski area in British Columbia, senior lift rates are approximately 15% less than regular adult lift rates and at Silverstar Mountain, also in BC, season passes for seniors are half the price of regular adult tickets. When arranging a ski outing, don't assume discounts are available only for lift tickets. Ask for all the senior discounts that apply.

The Mature Traveler, a monthly newsletter, carries lengthy lists of discounts in special categories. Their annual ski issue in November lists ski areas with their discount policies, phone numbers and websites. For back issues and subscription information, Tel. 800/460-6676, An organization for skiers who are aged 50 and more is Over the Hill Gang International, which has members in almost two dozen countries, offering discounts at 100 ski areas. The group also organizes ski trips for seniors. Tel. 719/389-0022, www.OTHGI.com.

Softball offers "a league of their own" for men aged 50 and better and women 45 and over. Divisions are organized by age groups in five-year increments up to those who are 70 and older. The league competes locally, regionally and nationally. There is probably a senior team near you. Contact SSUSA, suite 101A, 2701 K Street, Sacramento CA 95816, Tel. 916/326-5305, www.seniorsoftball.com.

Tennis competitions are organized by the United States Tennis Association for age groups in five-year increments starting at age 35 and ranging to age 90 for men and 80 and up for women. Membership in USTA is required. Tel. 914/696-7000, www.usta.com.

Warren River Expeditions is a whitewater adventure outfitter that caters to seniors. Book a trip for yourself or join one of the multi-generation groups of parents, kids and grandparents for an unforgettable ride on Idaho's Main Salmon River, Middle Fork of the Salmon River, and the Frank Church River of No Return. Nights are spent in comfortable, back-country lodges (unlike other trips that specialize in a younger crowd and bring only tents for overnight quarters). Fish for trout, explore the Sawtooth mountains, and run wild river chasms. Say you saw it in this book and a 10% discount applies to seniors ages 55 and better. One price buys rafting, lodging, guides and meals. Warren River Expeditions, Inc., Box 1375, Salmon, Idaho 83467, Tel. 208/756-6387 or 800/765-0421, www.raftidaho.com, e-mail SalmonRiver@RaftIdaho.com.

11. Discounts by Regions

Many cities or vacation regions offer a discount card, booklet or "pass" that entitles visitors to discounts at participating merchants, hotels, shops and restaurants. Often, locals don't even know about these bonanzas, which are usually free and available to anyone. Some are available by mail; others are free for the asking at turnpike rest areas and visitor information centers. Granted, many of the discounts are for hotel stays, which aren't of interest to locals, but you'll find many discounts on meals and purchases. If you haven't visited the Tourist Information Center in your home town, you'll be surprised at the deals you've been missing.

Even if you don't think of yourself as a senior citizen, call any local senior center if you're aged 50 or better and ask about local senior discounts. You may be entitled to a card, membership, list or newsletter that lists deals you never dreamed existed in your own backyard!

Whether you plan to visit the area or live there, here are some not-to-be missed deals:

Albuquerque, New Mexico has a citywide discount program on goods, services and restaurants for local seniors. Call your closest senior center and ask how to get the free card. You'll still have to contact businesses one by one to verify their discount policies, which vary by age and amount. Refresh your card regularly because new businesses join the list; others leave it.

Amherst, Massachusetts offers a string of senior discounts for goods and services, including restaurants, through the Council on Aging, www.ecommunityguideom/amherst/articles/seniorguide.

Boulder Colorado seniors take find city-wide discounts at www.bcn.boulder.co.us/community/senior-citizen/ Or, call any local senior center and ask about the program. Merchants volunteer senior discounts on many expenses from professional fees to auto repair. The list of participating merchants changes, and they all have their own rules about minimum age. If you're willing to do some spade work, there's money to be saved here.

Dare County, North Carolina (the Outer Banks) is a long strip of beach communities filled with nature sites, vacation homes, restaurants, museums, fishing charters, and history that goes back to Sir Walter Raleigh and the Lost Colony. The Outer Banks Getaway Card is available each year, free, and entitles the holder to discounts for whatever dates are requested. Offers aren't valid in peak summer months, but are issued for January 1-May 25 or September 15-December 31. You must present the card at the time of purchase. Discounts are based on availability and are subject to change, taxes, tips, and other restrictions. Order your card from Tel. 877/298-4373 or www.outerbanks.org. Participating businesses, which may change, are listed on the website.

Edmonton AB has a publication, Edmonton Senior, that publishes a list of all local businesses that offer a senior discount. Check with each individually for ages and amounts. Tel. 780/425-7463 or 866/425-3722, www.seniorsgotravel.com.

Mall of America in Bloomington MN is an entire city where one book of discounts applies to many different stores, services, entertainments, and places to eat.. Tel. 800/346-4289, www.bloomingtonmn.org for information on discount packages that include shopping, dining and accommodations.

New Hampshire's Lakes Region Factory Stores are a major destination for New England locals and visitors. Build a trip around the collection of 50 outlet stores, where seniors get a discount on Tuesdays. Arrive in town on a Monday evening, spend all day Tuesday shopping and having lunch at special savings, and don't leave town until Wednesday morning. Ask for the free Club Platinum Card at Easy Spirit in suite 220 or in the Management Office, suite 134. Fill out a simple form and receive a card good for fabulous deals and discounts at participating stores. Most discounts are 10-15% but every merchant's deal is different, including the inevitable fine print and exclusions. Stock up on Eddie Bauer, Springmaid-Wamsutta, Reebok, Brooks Brothers, Jones New York and many other brand names for yourself and gifts. Lakes Region Factory Stores, 120 Laconia Road, Tilton NH 03276, Tel. 603/286-7880.

Northwest residents can go to www.nw-seniorsonline.org for a growing list of discounts offered to people who live in Washington and Oregon.

Northern Ohio member hospitals of the ACMH hospital chain, which includes the internationally famous Cleveland Clinic, offer Senior Club membership to people aged 55 and over. Club members get discounts at hospital cafeterias and gift shops and on hearing aids, medical equipment and eyeglasses. Parking at the Cleveland Clinic is discounted, and members are also invited to free workshops and lectures. Tel. 440/997-6208, www.acmchealth.org/services/senior_circleplus.htm.

Ohioans save on thousands of goods and services statewide if they hold the Golden Buckeye Card, which is automatically sent to Ohio seniors at age 60. If you didn't get one, fill out an application at any public library or senior center. About 90 percent of the state's pharmacies offer a discount to card holders and thousands of other merchants voluntarily give senior discounts on goods and services of all kinds. Look for the Golden Buckeye logo as you enter the store. You'll have to show your signed card with each transaction. The list of participating merchants is found on the website. Ohio Department of Aging, 50 West Broad Street, Columbus OH 43215, Tel. 614/466-5500, www.state.oh.us/buckeye.

Orlando Magical Getaway Travel Club is open to Florida residents only, offering discounts and deals including last-minute bookings, discounted theme park admission, and much more. You'll have to show proof of residency, such as a Florida driver's license, when you check in. Because the deals change so often, the Club is available only online at www.orlandocvb.com. Regardless of where you live (including Orlando itself) any Orlando visit should begin with a stop at the Official Visitor Center for discount booklets and coupons galore. These deals are available to anyone.

St. Louis/St. Charles MO area seniors can join the Gateway Seniors Association, a non-profit group that screens businesses that offer a senior discount, and maintains an up-to-date list. Local seniors can get the list free, then search for the desired service. Businesses pay to participate. The long list includes accountants, attorneys, auto repair shops, heating/air conditioning companies, oral surgeons, kennels, moving and storage companies, picture framing, satellite television, photographers, ad inf. It's then up to you, the senior, to find a participating provider and sort out all the rules and details. Tel. 639/922-2551, www.gsainfo.org.

Seniors Today is a free newspaper found at supermarkets and shops throughout the Daytona Beach area. Pick it up when you're visiting Volusia or Flagler counties and page through it for coupons and senior perks. Senior newspapers and magazines like this one are found everywhere; many cities have two or three such publications, all of them free. Look for them in your city and when visiting elsewhere.

Texas State Parks give state residents aged 65 and older a Texas Parklands Passport that entitles them to a 50% discount, rounded off to the nearest whole dollar, on park entry fees. However, if you turned 65 before September 1, 1995, entry fees are waived completely! Veterans of the U.S. Armed Services holding a 60% or more service connected disability (as determined by the U.S. Veterans Administration) don't pay entry fees at those parks where entrance fees are collected.

Individuals who have been medically determined to be permanently disabled as as result of mental or physical impairment (including blindness) for purposes of receiving benefits under the Social Security Act and who are currently receiving those benefits will be entitled to 50% reduced entry rounded to the next whole dollar. Entry fees at state parks range from $1 to $5 per person for adults. Other fees, such as launch ramp, boat rental, and camping are additional.

Wisconsin Dells is one of the Midwest's most wondrous vacation spots. A long list of restaurants and shops participate in the Senior Discount Card program sponsored by Dells Boat Tours, Tel. 608/251-3381, extension 18, www.dellboats.com. If you're 55 or over, order the card before you go to the Dells and you'll save 10% and more in dozens of places.

STATE BY STATE

Here is contact information for every state's travel information. Ask specifically about senior discount brochures or booklets, policies regarding state park admission for seniors, and senior discounts on fishing and hunting licenses. Almost every state offers senior discounts for admission to state lands, some good for any senior and others available only to state residents. A few state tourism offices offer free booklets that focus on travel for seniors. In any case, ask whether senior-specific information is available. The more inquiries they log, the more these tourism authorities will realize the extent and influence of the senior travel dollar.

Alabama Bureau of Tourism & Travel
P.O. Box 4927
Montgomery AL 36103
Tel. 800/ALABAMA, www.touralabama.org.

Alaska Division of Tourism
P.O. Box 110801
Juneau AK 99811
Tel. 907/465-2010, www.dced.state.ka.us/tourism/

Arizona Office of Tourism
2702 North 3rd Street, Suite 4015
Phoenix AZ 85004
Tel. 602/230-7733, www.arizonaguide.com

Arkansas Department of Parks & Tourism
One Capitol Mall
Little Rock AR 72291
Tel. 800/NATURAL, www.arkansas.com

California Division of Tourism
P.O. Box 1499
Sacramento CA 95812
Tel. 800/862-2543, www.visitcalifornia.com

Colorado Tourism Office
1625 Broadway, Suite 1700
Denver CO 80202
Tel. 800/COLORADO or 303/892-3885, www.colorado.com

Connecticut Office of Tourism
505 Hudson Street
Hartford CT 06106
Tel. 800/CT-BOUND or 860/270-8080

Delaware Tourism Office
99 Kings Highway
Dover DE 19901
Tel. 866-2-VISIT-DE or 302/739-4272, www.visitdelaware.com.

District of Columbia Convention & Tourism Corporation
1212 New York Avenue SW #600
Washington DC 20005
Tel. 202/789-7000, www.washington.org

Florida Department of Environmental Protection, Parks Information
Mail Station 535, 3900 Commonwealth Boulevard
Tallahassee FL 32399
Tel. 850/488-9872, or for general information, 800/7FLA-USA, www.flausa.com. Campground and cabin reservations in state parks, 800/326-3521

Georgia Department of Tourism
285 Peachtree Center Avenue NE
Marquis Tower Two, Suite 1000
Atlanta GA 30303
Tel. 800/VISITGA or 404/656-3590, also www.gastateparks.org

Hawaii Visitors & Convention Bureau
2270 Kalakaua Avenue
Honolulu HI 96815
Tel. 808/924-0260, www.GoHawaii.com

Idaho Travel Council
P.O. Box 83720
Boise ID 83720
Tel. 800/VISIT-ID, www.visitid.com

Illinois Bureau of Tourism
100 West Randolph Street
Chicago IL 60602
Tel. 800/2-CONNECT, www.enjoyillinois.com

Indiana Tourism Division
1 North Capitol Street, Suite 700
Indianapolis IN 46204
Tel. 877/ENJOY-IN, www.enjoy.indiana.com

Iowa Division of Tourism
200 East Grand Avenue
Des Moines IA 50309
Tel. 800/345-IOWA or 515/242-705. www.traveliowa.com

Kansas Department of Tourism
1000 SW Jackson, Suite 100
Topeka KS 66612
Tel. 800/2-KANSAS or 785/296-2009, www.travelKS.com

Kentucky Department of Travel
P.O. Box 2011
Frankfurt KY 40602
Tel. 800/225-TRIP, extension 67, www.kentuckytourism.com

Maine Office of Tourism
33 Stone Street, 59 State House Station
Augusta ME 04333
Tel. 888/MAINE45, www.visitmaine.com

Maryland Office of Tourism
217 East Redwood Street
Baltimore MD 21202
Tel. 800/543-1036 or 410/767-3400, www.mdisfun.org

Massachusetts Office of Travel & Tourism
State Transportation Building
10 Park Plaza, Suite 4510

Boston MA 02116
Tel. 800/277-MASS, www.massvacation.com

Travel Michigan
4225 Miller Road, Suite 4
Flint MI 48507
Tel. 888/78-GREAT, www.michigan.org

Minnesota Office of Tourism
100 Metro Square
121 Seventh Place East
St. Paul MN 55101
Tel. 800/657-3700 or 651/296-5029, www.exploreminnesota.com.

Mississippi Division of Tourism
P.O. Box 1705
Ocean Springs MS 39566
Tel. 800/WARMEST, www.visitmississippi.org.

Missouri Division of Tourism
P.O. Box 1055
Jefferson City MO 65102
Tel. 573/751-4133, www.visitmo.com

Travel Montana
P.O. Box 200533 or 1424 9th Avenue
Helena MT 59620
Tel. 800/VISIT-MT or 406/444-2654, www.visitmt.com

New Hampshire Office of Travel & Tourism
Box 1856
Concord NH 03302
Tel. 603/271-2665 or 800/FUN-IN-NH, www.visitnh.gov

New Jersey Office of Tourism
P.O. Box 820 or 20 West State Street
Trenton NJ 08625
Tel. 800/VISIT-NJ or 609/292-2470, www.visitnj.org

New Mexico Department of Tourism
491 Old Santa Fe Trail
Santa Fe NM 87503
Tel. 800/SEE-NEW-MEX, www.newmexico.org

New York Division of Tourism
P.O. Box 2603
Albany NY 12222
Tel. 800/CALL-NYS or 518/474-4116, www.iloveny.com

Nevada Commission on Tourism
401 North Carson Street
Carson City NV 87901
Tel. 800/NEVADA or 775/687-4322, www.travelnevada.com

North Carolina Tourism Division
301 North Washington Street
Raleigh NC 27601
Tel. 800/VISIT-NC or 919/733-4171, www.visitnc.com

North Dakota Tourism
604 East Boulevard
Bismark ND 58505
Tel. 800/435-5663 or 701/328-2525, www.ndtourism.com

Ohio Division of Travel & Tourism
P.O. Box 1001
Columbus OH 43266
Tel. 800/BUCKEYE, www.ohiotourism.com

Oklahoma Tourism
P.O. Box 60789
Oklahoma City OK 73146
Tel. 800/652-6552 or 405/521-2409, www.travelOK.com

Oregon Parks & Recreation Department
1115 Commercial Street NE, Suite 1
Salem OR 97301
Tel. 503/378-6305 or 800/551-6949

Pennsylvania Office of Tourism
Commonwealth Keystone Building, 400 North Street, 4th Floor
Harrisburg PA 17120
Tel. 800/VISIT-PA or 717/787-5453, www.experiencepa.com

Rhode Island Tourism
One West Exchange Street
Providence RI 02903
Tel. 800/556-2484 or 401/222-2601, www.VisitRhodeIsland.com

South Dakota Department of Tourism
711 East Wells Avenue
Pierre SD 57501
Tel. 800/732-5682 or 605/773-3301, www.travelSD.com

Tennessee Tourism Development
320 Sixth Avenue North, 5th Floor, Rachel Jackson Building
Nashville TN 37243
Tel. 800/GO-2-TENN

Texas Tourism
P.O. Box 12728
Austin TX 78711
Tel. 800/888-8839, www.TravelTex.com

Utah Travel Council
Council Hall
Salt Lake City UT 84114
Tel. 800/200-1160 or 801/538-1030, www.utah.com

Vermont Department of Tourism and Marketing
6 Baldwin St., Drawer 33
Montpelier, VT 05633-1301
Tel. 800/VERMONT, www.1-800/VERMONT.com; email:
vttravel@dca.state.vt.us

Virginia Tourism Corporation
901 East Byrd Street
Richmond VA 23219
Tel. 800/932-5827, www.virginia.org

Washington Tourism Office
P.O. Box 42500
Olympia WA 98504
Tel. 800/544-1800 or 360/725-5050, www.experienceWashington.com

West Virginia Division of Tourism
201 East Washington Street East
Charleston WV 25305
Tel. 800/CALL-WVA, www.www.callwva.com

Wisconsin Department of Tourism
201 West Washington Avenue
Madison WI 53707
Tel. 800/432-TRIP, www.travelwisconsin.com. Also 800/373-2737 for travel information on Wisconsin and neighboring states

Wyoming Division of Tourism
I-25 at College Street
Cheyenne WY 82002
Tel. 800/225-5996 or 307/777-7777, www.wyomingtourism.org

U.S. Virgin Islands Department of Tourism
c/o Martin Public Relations
One Shockoe Plaza
Richmond VA 23219

CANADA
Travel Alberta
Box 2500
Edmonton AB T5J 2Z4

Canadian Heritage
Pacific & Yukon Region Office
Room 300, 300 West Georgia Street

Vancouver, British Columbia
Canada, V6B 6C6. Tel. 604/666-0176. Contact this office for information on parks in British Columbia and the Yukon.

Travel Manitoba
7th Floor, 155 Carlton Street
Winnipeg MB R3C 3H8
Tel. 800/665-0040, www.travelmanitoba.com

New Brunswick Tourism
P.O. Box 12345
Woodstock NB EOJ 2BO
Tel. 800/561-0123 or 204/945-3777, www.tourismnbcanada.com

Newfoundland and Labrador Tourism
P.O. Box 8730
St. John's NF AIB 4K2
Tel.800/563-6353 or 709/729-2830, www.gov.nf.ca/tourism

Nova Scotia Tourism
World Trade & Convention Center
1800 Argyle Street
Halifax NS B3J 2R7
Tel. 800/565-0000 or 902-424-5000, www.explore.gov.ca/virtualns.com

Ontario Ministry of Tourism
Queen's Park
Toronto ON M7A 1C6
Tel. 800/ONTARIO, www.tourism-toronto.com, www.rainbowcountry,com, www.ontarionorth.com, www.ontarioeast.com

Prince Edward Island Tourism
129 Queen Street
Charlottetown PEI C1A 4B3
Tel. 877/MEET-PEI or 902/368-3688, www.meetingspei.com

Tourism Saskatchewan
1922 Park Street

Regina Saskatchewan S4P 3V7
Tel. 306-787-2300 or 877-ESCAPE, www.sasktourism.com

Tourism Quebec
P.O. Box 979
Montreal QE H3C 2W3
Tel. 514-864-3838, www.bonjour-quebec.com

If you're driving the Alaska Highway, the following group promotes tourism along the route in Alaska, Yukon, British Columbia, and Alberta. Senior discounts are available in many parks, campgrounds, motels and restaurants along the way. Contact:
Tourism North
c/o The Alaska Travel Industry Association
2600 Cordova Street, Suite 201
Anchorage AK 99503
Tel. 800/862-5275, www.northtoalaska.com

When in Rome

You'll spend more than necessary in foreign countries unless you know that:

• Water is not provided free with meals in most countries outside North America. If you ask for water, you may be served bottled water and charged a hefty price for it. In many regions including much of Europe, bread is not always served free with a meal. Order it and you'll be charged.

• In parts of the world, there is a charge for sitting down at a table. That's why you'll see many diners standing up around small counters to have a sandwich or a breakfast croissant.

• Tipping is uncommon in some cultures and unknown in others. In many countries, a service charge of 10-20%, is added to every hotel and restaurant bill. Don't insult the server by tipping in a culture where it's not done or don't start a trend by tipping where it is not expected, such as when snapping a local person's picture. Lastly, don't tip again (except in cases where a special services has been done for you) if a service charge has been added to your bill.

MEXICO
Mexican Consulate
610 A Street
San Diego CA 92101
619/231-8414

Mexican Tourism, Tel. 800/44-MEXICO. Also contact the Discover Baja Travel Club, Tel. 800/727-BAJA or the Vagabundos Del Mar Travel Club, Tel. 800/474-BAJA.

BERMUDA
Bermuda sponsors Golden Rendezvous Month each February, inviting travelers who are 50 and over to endless rounds of activities, lectures, bus tours and museum events, most of them free. The program is different every year so put Bermuda, which is only a two-hour flight from the eastern United States, on your spring travel schedule. It's an island of two seasons, Spring and Summer, where our winter is their discount season and accommodations sell for half the high-season price. Bermuda is a natural for golfers, yachties, divers, shoppers, and beach-goers, but there is something here for everyone from history buffs to couch potatoes who simply want a gracious getaway in an island locale. Contact Bermuda Tourism, Tel. 800/BER-MUDA, www.bermudatourism.com.

OTHER NATIONS
When you're traveling abroad, keep an eye peeled for senior discounts but don't expect them to be the same as those found in North America. Age limits may be higher, usually starting at 65 and older. Senior discounts are most common at hotels, for admission to attractions and museums, and on air, rail or bus fares.

Australia: Destination Queensland
c/o Fontayne Group
430 Colorado Avenue
Santa Monica CA 90401, www.visitbrisbane.com

Belgian Tourist Office
780 Third Avenue #1501
New York NY 10017
www.visitbelgelgium.com

British Tourist Authority
515 Fifth Avenue #701
New York NY 10176
www.travelbritain.org

Caribbean Travel Organization
c/o Kahn Travel Communications
77 North Centre (stet) Avenue #215
Rockville Centre NY 11570

Danish Tourism Board
655 Third Avenue, 18th Floor
New York NY 10017
www.visitdenmark.com

Finnish Tourism Board
655 Third Avenue
New York 10017

French Government Tourist Office
444 Madison Avenue, 16th Floor
New York NY 10022
www.francetourism.com

German National Tourism Office
122 West 42nd Street, 52nd Floor
New York NY 10168
www.germany-tourism.de

Israel Ministry of Tourism
800 Second Avenue
New York NY 10017

Japan National Tourism Organization
One Rockefeller Plaza #1250
New York NY 10020
www.jntonyc.com

Netherlands Board of Tourism
355 Lexington Avenue, 19th Floor
New York NY 10017
Tel. 888/GO-HOLLAND
www.goholland.com

New Zealand Tourism Board
501 Santa Monica Boulevard, Suite 300
Santa Monica CA 90401
Tel. 866/NEW ZEALAND
www.tourisminfo.govt.nz

Norwegian Tourist Board
655 Third Avenue, Suite 1810
New York NY 10017
Tel. 212/885-9757
www.norway.org

Portuguese Travel & Tourism Commission
60 Bloor Street West #1005
Toronto ON M4W 3B8
Tel. 416/921-7376

South African Tourism
500 Fifth Avenue
New York NY 10110-0002
www.southafrica.net

Tourist Office of Spain
666 Fifth Avenue, 35th Floor
New York NY 10103
www.okspain.org

Switzerland Tourism
608 Fifth Avenue
New York NY 10019
www.switzerlandtourism.com

Index

INDEX

FANTASTIC DISCOUNTS & DEALS FOR ANYONE OVER 50!

Comments Please!

Things change, so we welcome your comments to keep this book up to date. If you come across any new information, we'd appreciate hearing from you. No item is too small! Drop us an email note at: Jopenroad@aol.com, or write us at:

Fantastic Discounts
Cold Spring Press
P.O. Box 284
Cold Spring Harbor, NY 11724

We offer bulk purchases at significant discounts. If you are interested in buying this book in quantity, contact us at the address below for more details.

Cold Spring Press
P.O. Box 284, Cold Spring Harbor, NY 11724
E-mail: Jopenroad@aol.com

For US orders, include $4.00 for postage and handling for the first book ordered; for each additional book, add $1.00. Orders outside US, inquire first about shipping charges (money order payable in US dollars on US banks only for overseas shipments).